THE AMERICAN MARTIAL ARTS ALLIANCE FOUNDATION

MARTIAL ARTS EXTRAORDINAIRE
BIOGRAPHY BOOK

50 YEARS
OF MARTIAL ARTS
Excellence

By

GRAND MASTER JESSIE BOWEN

All attempts have been made to ensure the accuracy of the information presented in this book, but this is not a guarantee.

Publisher: Elite Publications

First Printing of Vol. 6: July 2021

Language: English

Paperback ISBN-13: 978-1-7368338-8-9

Hardcover ISNB-13: 978-1-7368338-9-6

Elite Publications, 2120 E Firetower Rd #107-58, Greenville, NC 27858

http://www.elitepublications.org

Ordering Information: Special discounts are available on quantity purchases by corporations, associations, educators, and others. For details, contact the publisher at the above address U.S. trade bookstores and wholesalers: Please contact Jessie Bowen.
Tel: (919) 618-8075 or email info@elitepublications.org

THE AMERICAN MARTIAL ARTS ALLIANCE FOUNDATION

MARTIAL ARTS EXTRAORDINAIRE

BIOGRAPHY BOOK

50 YEARS OF MARTIAL ARTS EXCELLENCE

Publisher:

Elite Publications

2120 E Firetower Rd #107-58

Greenville, NC 27858

www.elitepublications.org

Content Editors:

Grand Master Jessie Bowen

Jessica C. Phillips

Krystal L. Harvey

Associate Editor:

Gwendolyn Bowen

Marketing Coordinator:

Jessica C. Phillips

Interior Design & Book Cover:

Krystal L. Harvey

Tiger Shark, Inc.

www.tigersharkmediausa.com

Contributors:

Jan Wellendorf

Darrell Simms

Randy Robinson

Daryl Stewart

Stephen K. Hayes

TABLE OF CONTENTS

Acknowledgements

I want to convey my heartfelt gratitude to Jan Wellendorf, my Martial Arts instructor, who has influenced me as a martial artist and author.

Thank you to Grandmaster Ron Van Clief and the other martial artists who have contributed to the publication of this book by entrusting their biographical material.

The Martial Arts Extraordinaire Biography book gives us a glimpse into their personal lives. I want to thank Jessica Phillips and Krystal Harvey for their tireless efforts in putting this excellent book together.

Finally, Gwendolyn Bowen, my lovely and supportive wife, I want to convey my heartfelt gratitude for your words of encouragement as we faced our many challenges.

Grand Master Jessie Bowen
American Martial Arts Alliance Foundation
Elite Publishing

50 YEARS OF MARTIAL ARTS EXCELLENCE

Foreword

The journey of a thousand miles begins with one step. "Lao Tzu" This quote represents the martial artist featured in the Martial Arts Extraordinaire Biography book. They are one-of-a-kind men and women who have dedicated their lives to the study of martial arts for more than 50 years.

The Martial Arts Extraordinaire Biography is the first book of its kind to highlight martial artists who have studied for fifty years or more. We want to express our gratitude to the men and women featured in this historical publication for allowing us to accompany them on their martial arts journey for more than half a century.

The inspiration for this book originated from a Facebook post by Grandmaster Ron Van Clief, who had been posting about his organization's founding for over 50 years. So, I started asking how many other martial artists have been studying martial arts for this amount of time. Grandmaster Ron Van Clief, recognized for motivating people through his action films and his dedication to martial arts development and improvement. It is an honor to dedicate this book to his memory and the countless men and women who have been motivated to continue their martial arts training due to his efforts. He is most renowned for inspiring us with his action flicks and his commitment to the growth and progress of martial arts. As you can see, martial arts is still a relatively new phenomenon in the United States, dating back to the early 1940s. However, these men and women paid their dues and should be called exceptional martial artists from the 1960s and 1970s.

Reading the biographies in the Martial Arts Extraordinaire Biography book provides us with insights into each life experience and helps us achieve our martial arts goals.

Darrell Simms, Randy Robinson, Daryl Stewart, and Jan Wellendorf, members of the American Martial Arts Alliance Board of Advisors, deserve special recognition for their support and encouragement.

Grand Master Jessie Bowen

American Martial Arts Foundation

Elite Publications

Introduction & Dedication

I began my study of Karate in 1963 at the age of 23 at the Ohio Judo Association in Cleveland, Ohio. The karate program was run by a guy fresh from the Marine base on Okinawa. The training program was so hard that all I wanted to do was reach green belt, then quit. When I said it was tough, that's what I meant; I went to the hospital four times before I got my green belt.

Of course, by that time, I was almost committed - almost. It didn't get any easier; I just got better bandages. I also first met Dale Brooks (my soon-to-be business partner) in 1963; he was the owner of the Judo school to which we all belonged. He was having a fundraiser at the old West Side school in Cleveland, Ohio. I went along for the ride. Mr. Brooks presented a proposal to buy "debentures," and according to him, it would get us (the Dojo) out of debt. From the time I met him, almost to the day he died, he never stopped trying to raise money for one cause or another.

The story of how Karate International started is a good one to know. By early 1969 the school was named The Ohio Judo and Karate Association, and I worked full time at the Dojo. We worked for a year on how to create a direct sales method of selling our courses in the home door-to-door. We had failed at everything we tried. Finally, Dale threw up his hands and exclaimed, "That's it. I give up. I'm just not putting any more time or money into this." That's when I said, "Can I have it?" I don't know where it came from; I just said it. But the instant I did say it, I knew it was right. Dale answered, "Go on, take it, I want nothing to do with it. I'm not spending another dime." So, I took the job. A week later, I walked into Dale's office and handed him a contract.

When I got the inspiration to ask for the rights to sell the course - I knew I could do it. A week later, I gave Dale a contract and $300.00. I knew I had a winner. At that point, I shook Dale's hand and said, "This is it. I'm saying goodbye." Dale responded, "What do you mean, good-bye?" I said, "I'm leaving to sell courses to every karate school in the country." I actually had my hand on the doorknob to his office when he told me, "Hey, wait! Whatever you can do alone, you can do better with me." I answered, "You're right, but it will cost you half of what you own and half of what you'll ever own." He replied, "DONE!" We shook hands and have been partners ever since then.

Moving up in time, I opened the doors of Karate International in Raleigh in 1974. Jessie Bowen and Rob Olevsky came along in the mid-'70s and were immediate tournament champions. Rob eventually focused on building schools while Jessie focused on the tournament environment, winning or placing at nearly all local and national events.

One of the purposes of my writing this introduction for Mr. Bowen is to say that he is one of the finest men and martial artists I have ever known, bar-none. He survived when others failed. He overcame when others gave way. I am truly honored to know him and call him not just a student but also a friend. And to the others who appear in this book, I wish you all the best. You are the ones who carry the torch. It is up to you to carry the honor that goes with your appearance herein.

O'Sensei Jan Wellendorf
10th Degree Black Belt
Founder of Karate International

50 YEARS OF MARTIAL ARTS EXCELLENCE

THE FOUNDATION OF MARTIAL ARTS IN AMERICA

In the beginning, American martial artists got their start with military folks in Japan after WWII and Korea after the Korean War. Remember those days, when the martial arts were a rare and exotic thing, and people who studied them were regarded as adventure seekers?

Asian masters took pride in seeing Americans take to their arts and earn rank. They quickly agreed to the American military people's requests to take those Asian arts home with them to teach when they returned stateside after serving. Thus, was born the American fascination with the Asian martial arts.

Those original martial arts pioneers generally kept the flavor of their arts' home country. Classes were taught with the arts' original language, garb, and culture. Diplomas were issued and sent over from the art's headquarters in Asia. White gis, colored belts, and bowing were unquestioned parts of the package.

Those original 1950s teachers produced a next generation of students who took to the Asian martial arts. Americans famously sportified the arts, making competition a growing part of the practice. American boxing and wrestling sneaked their way into some martial arts schools. Other schools retained a strict Asian approach. A wide range of practice developed in the USA, and many styles and approaches came to be.

An eventual third and even fourth generation matured in the arts. Sometimes the arts were preserved in their very Asian way. Sometimes the arts were so Americanized that they had no Asian influence to be seen in them at all.

Now it is time to celebrate those noble original followers of the martial arts in America, the ones who produced teachers who went on to create even more teachers. These are men and women who for more than 50 years have devoted their lives, passions, and commitment to the development of others through martial arts. Once we all were juniors, young and strong, striving to earn those first degrees of Black Belt, battling it out in competitions, founding associations of the like-minded. Now we have become the white-haired elders, the establishers of legacy to be carried on after us by our students and their students.

How amazing it is that anyone could devote an entire lifetime to martial arts endeavor. Many spent their years maturing in technique, uncovering secrets that their original instructors surreptitiously planted in their lessons. Many moved from art to art, as their expertise grew and their curiosity took them on to new experiences. Some founded great dynasties of multi-school associations. Some stayed in small borrowed facilities, teaching but a few dedicated students. Some earned great fame and financial wealth. Others worked day jobs just to be able to teach a few evenings per week. Some have happy memories of a close parent to child relationship with their old teacher, where true caring lifted them to heights of personal development. Some remember having to leave a teacher, summoning a new loyalty to their own potential in the art.

We each of us have lived our unique stories in the martial arts. We celebrated our triumphs. We struggled through our challenges. We made it, somehow. We began with hundreds of others who faltered and quit along the way. Now we are the elders, the ones who held fast to our life-long search for martial truth.

Relish this book. Read every story, even those of persons you are not familiar with. Look for the common shared experiences we all went through. Then look for those unique parts to each story. What has that specific person gained from their lifetime in the martial arts? What did he or she have to give up in order to become a now revered elder? Did he or she ever consider just throwing in the towel and quitting? What were the breakthrough moments that sealed-in the commitment that leads to a lifelong career? What did it take to move from anonymous beginner so many years ago to becoming a revered and celebrated elder in the martial arts?

With this book, we celebrate those outstanding persons who have spent over 50 years in the martial arts. My congratulations to every person represented herein. You made it! We all started out with lesson one, and now we are acknowledging each other as fellow life-long followers of the path. I am proud to be included in such a grand collection of noble spirits!

An-shu Stephen K. Hayes

Member Black Belt Hall of Fame 1985

2015 Recipient of MAIA Lifetime Achievement Award

Founder To-Shin Do Ninja Martial Arts

StephenKHayes.com

THE AMERICAN MARTIAL ARTS ALLIANCE FOUNDATION

50 YEARS OF MARTIAL ARTS EXCELLENCE

INTRODUCTION TO THE WHO'S WHO BOOK SERIES

The Who's Who Book Series is not intended to be just another martial arts book. It is intended to be both inspirational and motivational as you discover martial artists whose lives have been changed through the study of an application of the principles taught in the martial arts.

For more than 1500 years, martial arts has played a key role in personal development training and through the pages of this book you will discover the journey of hundreds of martial artists sharing their journeys, describing how the martial arts has impacted their lives.

Grand Master Bowen's Changing Lives Edition represents the shift we Americans have brought to the arts, by recognizing the accomplishments of the individuals who practiced and perfected their arts, as opposed to the glorification of the arts themselves. In reading about what the Martial Arts Masters & Pioneers Leaders here have done, one can only marvel at the magnitude of individual effort expended and sacrifices made, from the grassroots activities to global media and organizational results.

So, rather than debating which blocks or strikes or styles are more perfect, this work heralds the individual strengths of those who share the marital bond in America, whose legacies have impacted martial arts in America and thus, around the world.

No matter where you are in life, the martial arts offer a powerful tool to aid you physically, mentally and spiritually as your mind and body work better together. The study of the martial arts helps individuals look inside and find their purpose. Along the path, they discover how to let go of the negativity and the things that hold them back in life. Enjoy here the journeys of Masters & Pioneers.

THE AMERICAN MARTIAL ARTS ALLIANCE FOUNDATION

50 YEARS OF MARTIAL ARTS EXCELLENCE

HONORS

GRAND MASTER RON "THE BLACK DRAGON" VAN CLIEF

I started studying martial arts with GM Moses Powell and GM Ronald Duncan at the St. John's Community Center in Brooklyn circa 1959. As a teenager, I became a fan of martial arts movies. So my brother, Pete, and I would hop on the train to Chinatown. In 1960, I met GM Peter Urban and became his student until I joined the U.S. Marine Corps (1960-1966). While in the Marine Corps, I studied karate in Okinawa and in the Philippines. I was mentored by GM Remy Presas, GM Leung Ting, GM Duncan Leung, GM Ron Taganashi, Frank Ruiz, Harry Rosenstein, George Cofield, GM Danny K. Pai, GM Ed Parker, GM Steve Muhammad, GM Bruce Lee, GM Relson Gracie, and Gary Alexander.

Martial arts has changed my entire life. It's become my way of life. It is the best people builder, personal development, and character developer in my life. I am grateful to continue my journey and spread the knowledge and spirit of true martial arts.

MARTIAL ARTS STYES & RANKS:

- Sanuces - Black belt
- Shotokan Karate - 5th Dan
- American Goju - 9th Dan
- TKD - 2nd Dan
- Aikijitsu - 8th Dan
- Wing chun - student
- Wing tsun - student
- Modern Arnis Lakan Pito
- Relson Gracie Jiu-jitsu - Purple Belt

INSTRUCTORS:

- GM Moses Powell
- GM Ronald Duncan

- GM RON Taganashi
- GM Frank Ruiz
- GM Harry Rosenstein
- GM George Cofield
- GM S Henry Cho
- GM Remy Presas
- GM Duncan Leung
- GM Relson Gracie
- Prof Ronn Shiraki

PROFESSIONAL ORGANIZATIONS:

- Screen Actor Guild (AFTRA)
- East Coast Stuntmen's Association
- Chung Wah Athletic Association
- Chinese Goju International
- International Sports hall of Fame

- Negro Ensemble Company

PERSONAL ACHIEVEMENTS:

- Martial Arts Champion 5 time World Karate Champion
- 15 time All American Champion
- Black Belt Magazine Hall of Fame
- First Foreigner to Headline Hong Kong Movies 1974
- Senior combative for the United States Secret Service 1983-1993 at NY World Trade Center
- USMC honorable discharge 1966
- New York City transit police officer 1965-1969

MAJOR ACHIVEMENTS:

- Author of Manual of the Martial Arts, The Ron Van Clief Guidebooks White Belt to Black Belt, Black Heroes of the Martial Arts, Vol 1, 2 and 3, The Hanged Man, Sentences the Tao of the Black Dragon
- Competed in over 900 tournaments in 57 years of

MAJOR ACHIVEMENTS:

- Fought in UFC 4 at the age of 51 yrs old. Oldest fighter to ever fight in the history of the UFC and former Commissioner of the UFC 1995-1996.
- Trained over 500,000 students worldwide.
- Founded The Chinese Goju System and Black Dragon Aikijitsu System in 1971.
- Started competing in Brazilian Jiu-jitsu at the age of 71. Last competed at age of 77.
- Produced the documentary The Hanged Man in 2020.
- Presently in post-production on the documentary Super Weapon 2.
- Finishing a four-volume set of Black Heroes of the Martial Arts
- Worked as a stunt man for three decades and a member of the stunt committee.
- Worked on over 100 films, television, and cable programs.
- Presently training in Relson Gracie Jiujitsu at the age of 78.

Melvin Armstrong

> "I learned and understood that having great character, faith, integrity, courage, dedication, hard work, and perseverance can help achieve any goal."

Martial arts has impacted my life tremendously in health and career. From my nine aunts and uncles and my four siblings who had a God faith base, I learned and understood that having great character, faith, integrity, courage, dedication, hard work, and perseverance can help achieve any goal. Growing up, I did not have much patience, took things for granted, and reacted without thinking of the consequences because I had an incredible support group.

By assisting me in understanding the why, where, when, and what of my home training, Sifu repeated and complemented my previous childhood teachings. In my younger years, I simply did things on the spur of the moment, taking life, friends, and people for granted.

During my two years of Sifu's Master's training, I learned to be more patient, alert, tolerable, conscientious, confident, and aware in dealing with physical and life issues, obnoxious people, and things. I also learned how

TRAINING INFORMATION

- Martial Arts Styles & Ranks: Boxing, Shotokan (Purple Belt), Kenpo (White Belt), Southern Shaolin 5-Animal/5-Family Kung Fu (Masters Black Sash
- Instructors/Influencers: Sensei Bruce Tegner, Sensei Chuck Sullivan, Sifu Wong Ark Yuey
- Birthdate: December 16, 1936
- Birthplace/Growing Up: Springfield, OH
- Yrs. In the Martial Arts: 67 years
- Yrs. Instructing: 51 years
- School Owner & Instructor at Armstrong's Southern Shaolin Kung Fu (now closed and instructing privately)

PROFESSIONAL ORGANIZATIONS

- Data Processing Association
- AARP State Legislation Team
- Alliance Lifetime Member
- The Columbus Ohio World Of Martial Hall Of Fame

to read people and things before they happened, that there are always two sides to every story, be responsive rather than reactive when resolving issues, and just be more effective in all walks of life.

BIO

After some conversations with my friend, Davey Moore, who was the Featherweight Champion of the World at the time, I started martial arts in 1954 by doing some boxing at the Springfield, Ohio, YMCA.

After reading a Mas Oyama karate book in 1961, I decided that I wanted to learn karate. I discovered that the white YMCA was offering karate classes, but the instructor was not permitted to teach at our YMCA due to the city's segregation, and we were not permitted to attend the white YMCA. Their Judo instructor was allowed to teach Judo at our YWCA in 1963, and I took some Judo classes there.

I went to the LA area around Inglewood in early 1963 in search of a career change. I began looking for a karate studio along the Hollywood Freeway after settling into a night job at the Long Beach Naval Shipyard. Bruce Tegner's Shotokan school was only two blocks from the Hollywood Freeway.

I earned a purple belt after four months of study with Bruce Tegner, but the training was not what I had read in Oyama's book. So, I quit and went to an Ed Parker Kenpo school on Crenshaw Blvd, which was closer to my house. Chuck Sullivan, the instructor, was fantastic.

PROFESSIONAL ORGANIZATIONS

- Whipping Willow Association
- Wah Que Kung Fu Center (Certification of Affiliation)
- Carmel Police Citizens Academy
- Council Elder for the Catawba Carrs-Run Ohio Indian Tribe

PERSONAL ACHIEVEMENTS

- Elder in the Carrs-Run Ohio Catawba Indian Tribe.
- Retired from Federal Government in 2007.
- Retired from Accenture as an IT consultant/ contractor in 2010
- Active community volunteer
- Church Officer
- Owner of Reel Computer Consultant, Inc.
- Owner of Armstrong's Kung-fu Academy Martial Arts training and retail business.
- Vice President for the Indianapolis Chapter of Indiana Black Expo
- Candidate for a South Bend School Board Trustee position.
- Worked with at risk students within the South Bend School System.
- On-shore IT manager for the AT&T U-Verse development
- Pictured on the cover of the book: 'Secrets of Kung-fu'.
- IUPUI College Student Mentor.
- Past Microsoft Partner
- Writing to publish My Martial Arts Journey

Because I may possibly compete in tournaments, I appreciated the sparring and excitement in the training. Going into the door, taking off your shoes, bowing, going to the dressing area, hitting the padded post until your hands were scared, returning to the mat, bowing, and fighting until you won or lost were all part of the training. I like it, but I had two issues: my hands were constantly hurting, which was a problem in my computer career, and I saw Ed Parker select his pupils in an unethical way for his Long Beach Tournament. Chuck was able to help me with my hand condition by having me hold a matchstick while sparring. Regardless, I started looking for another karate school.

During my search for a school, I visited a Japanese karate school of the renowned Japanese instructor named Nishiyama, but he told me that he only competes in Japanese-sanctioned tournaments. Since I wanted to compete against other martial arts, I decided to continue looking.

For help, I contacted a Black Belt Magazine staff member who asked me about my objective. I said to be a Black Belt. He suggested purchasing a Black Belt Certificate from them for $500. I did not know whether he was playing or not. But I told him that I wanted to earn my belt. Being surprised, I asked about Chinese teachers, which I saw in the phone book. I was warned to stay away from the Chinese arts because they were too dangerous—this sounded interesting. So, I looked in Chinatown for a teacher.

MAJOR ACHIEVEMENTS

- North Central College and University Accreditation Team.
- CEO for South Bend, IN, Headstart Program.
- Officer in Kiwanis, Toastmasters, and Junior Achievement.
- United Way Representative for Northern Indiana Colleges and Universities.
- Received the 'State of Indiana Excellence in Teaching' award.
- Assisted Congressman Hinkley resolving the Election Fraud and Scam.
- Discovered how an Election committed election fraud was committed.
- One of 18 people on the National Election Watch Team.
- Assisted U.S. Watergate Attorneys and OIG on the U.S Grain Fraud project,
- Federal Civil Rights Officer.
- 1987 International Summer Special Olympics Games Volunteer.
- Adjunct IT Professor at Notre Dame University and Ancilla College.
- Manager for Inmates IT program at the Leavenworth Federal Penitentiary.
- South Bend and the Carmel School Board Diversity team Member.
- Trained as a National Disaster Preparedness and Response team.
- National Conference of Bankruptcy Clerks Member.
- Member of the Carmel, IN, Police Citizen Academy Advisor
- Carmel Police Citizen Community Advisory Academy member.
- State AARP Legislative Team.

One evening in 1964, I found a Chinese Kung-Fu studio in Chinatown above a rowdy bar named 'Wah Que.' The name on the door was 'Wong Ark Yuey.' After going upstairs, I saw an older Chinese gentleman with his back facing the students and reading a newspaper. Then he came onto the floor and started teaching. About ½ hour later, he read his paper, and a student took over the class. I noticed other strange things. There was no sparring; students were practicing strange moves and patterns; they used strange-looking weapons, stood around talking, and worked out in street clothes. Some wore suits that looked like pajamas, and they wore shoes. They were sticking their hands into a slow cooker, then stabbing into buckets, and hitting and pushing different-sized punching bags. I heard no noise such as Ki-I's when punching. However, even though all of this appeared strange, for some reason, I was still highly intrigued by everything I saw.

Then one evening, after sitting and watching these classes for approximately five weeks, I decided this was not the type of martial arts school I was looking for. As I was leaving, the old Chinese man came over to me and asked me to wait until he locked the downstairs door. Upon returning, he sat next to me and said: 'I want to teach you my 5-Animal/5-Family Kung-Fu'. At this time, I had no idea how honored I was to be personally told by a Chinese Master that he wanted to teach his Kung Fu Family's System. In fact, as of today, I have found no other student who was ever told this.

The remainder of my story will be presented in 3 parts:

BIO (continued)

1964 – 1966 (Core/Basic Training), 1966 – 1968 (Masters Training), and 1968 to the Present.

From 1964 – 1966 (Core/Basic Training): This training consisted of learning Sifu's personal Family Kung Fu System basics. Because of my limited training time, approximately 90% of my training was done 1-on-1 by Sifu himself. I attended regular classes whenever I could for 10% of my training. He gave me a key to help my training, then had me come to his store, take a nap on his backroom cot, get me some food, and bring me to the school where he trained me behind locked doors.

During my first 4/5 weeks, Sifu stood me in the North East corner of the room and positioned me on a strong Horse stance where I stood in puddles of my sweat and sore legs, thinking why I am not learning Kung Fu not knowing this was an honor for Sifu to be personally training me.

I had no idea the honor and the importance of this special attention while at the same time questioning myself as to why I am paying money to stand in a corner when I wanted to learn Kung-Fu.

After Sifu saw that my horse stance was strong enough to start my next training phase, he had me walk back-and-forth on 10 yards long white tape pasted on the floor at 45 -degree angles and a straight line. He worked me on the 3-arm sectional Cows Horn, walking the Cat and the Horse on Angels and Straight lines, crossing the legs, walking in Circles, transiting between the Cat and Horse stances as I was walking, punching and wiping-off to speed my hands, circling the wrists for flexibility and palm pushing exercises. He worked with me increasing my hand speed and soft (hand of Cotton) and hard blocks. After this, he moved me to soaking my hands in a crockpot of hot hand medicine before using the wooden arm dummy and punching and pushing a set of 6 hard and soft bags, and poking/jabbing into buckets of Peas, Rice, Gravel, and Sand.

After sharpening my basic skills, Sifu allowed me to join a regular class where I worked on stretching while learning his developed 'Wong Ga Kuen' (Wong Family Fist). In Cantonese, 'Ga' means 'Family' and 'Kuen' means 'Fist,' also known as 'Kung Fu and' Hands.' I learned the Basic/ Core 5-Animals (Dragon for agility, Crane for balance, Leopard for power, Tiger for bone strength, and Snake for Chi) and Hung Ga. I also learned his 2-Man and Weapon acting/sets, special Salute, Core Acting/Sets, weapons,

BIO (continued)

Lion Dancing, and Self-defense for demonstrations.

1966 – 1968 (Masters Training): In 1966, Sifu said: 'I want to teach you my Masters Training.' He told me that the Master training is unique for every Master training. My classes were on Wednesday evenings for 1 hour each at a cost between $35 and $50 for the Animals (more than 5), the 5 Fighting/Boxing Family's (Choy Ga, Fut Ga (the Monks Hands), Li Ga, Hung Ga (long-range boxing), and Mok (in close boxing), and many weapons. Each training was exceptionally longer than the Core training because I was trained to develop my own personal Kung Fu Family (Armstrong Ga Kuen). There was no discussion and explanation because it was up to each trained Master to develop their own family of movements and patterns. There was no recapping of previous sessions. And I was told not to practice my Master's training in front of anyone. He did tell me that I would know who was given Master's training. After each session, we did breathing exercises.

Sifu told me that his style was a strong Horse, Fast Hands, and a Countering system. He said that 'you cannot win a battle unless you go into battle on a strong horse.' He said to hit the same spot with Live Hands before they moved. He said to watch for them to blink then hit them because most people get knocked out when they blink. I learned some Internal training and the basics of effective torquing for power. He said to hit the same spot with Live Hands before they moved. He said to watch for them to blink then hit them because most people get knocked out when they blink. I learned some Internal training and the basics of effective torquing for power. He said to move your head and to move on angles. He said his system was like American Boxing with his acting/sets like American Shadow Boxing. He said the Family Boxing Fists, Choy, Fut, Hung, Li, and Mok are the most important things to learn for Self-defense purposes. He said learning the Animals trains your instincts, alertness, awareness, and your 5 Senses, and trains your 6th sense used to feel things before things happen.

From 1968 to the Present: Sifu used this time to perfect my Master's training, understanding, and how to be an Heir to his system. He told me that he wanted me to be his personal assistant, help him publish his second book, and asked me to open a school in the area. All of these were three of the greatest honors I ever received. After Sifu awarded me my Master's Certificate in a brief ceremony and ceremoniously wrapped and tied my Black Sash around me, the very next day, it seemed like a dam of trust opened, and a great relationship started between Sifu and me. He shared some very personal things with me, such as how and who to train. Some things were so personal; I decided to take them to my grave. I drove Sifu between LA and Frisco. In Frisco, he took me into the Hop Sing Tong Association and to some of his friend's schools, where he introduced me as his assistant. He was

BIO (continued)

challenged twice and called on me to fight for him. He said: 'if you beat Melvin, I will fight you.' Having not spared in a long time, I was stunned. But I had enough faith in him, knowing that he knows something about me that I did not know. And, I had no problem with either opponent. He tested me in other ways on several occasions. In October of 1970, the government transferred me to Washington, DC. Today, I teach and talk as Sifu taught and trained me.

Lawrence Arthur

"Each step was first a dream, a goal, all part of a journey, into tomorrow's dreams."

BIO

Not unlike many other great masters and innovators of the art of karate, Grand Master Lawrence Arthur has conceptualized and painstakingly developed "The American Freestyle Karate System". In 1976, after almost a decade of experience and dedicated devotion to the study of martial arts, Master Arthur originated "American Freestyle Karate". Master Arthur's formidable background in the martial arts included the study of Tae Kwon Do, Tang Soo Do, Karate, Kobudo, Judo, Aikido, Bando, American Boxing and Kickboxing. Taking the best techniques from each of these highly respected art forms, he incorporated them into a unique system which allowed for growth and improvement. This concept was very much different than that taught by traditional martial arts philosophies.

To further his skills and knowledge, Master Arthur began training in full contact karate and kickboxing. Through

TRAINING INFORMATION

- Instructors/Influencers: Don Mike Davis, h G.T. Massie, Walter Chen, Joe Gutowski
- Yrs. In the Martial Arts: 53 years

PERSONAL & MAJOR ACHIEVEMENTS

- 1969 Started training to fight "Full Contact Karate" (before there was kickboxing)
- 1972 Received 1st Degree Black Belt through the American Taekwondo Association (ATA).
- 1976 Opened first school, the American Taekwondo Academy in Lynchburg, VA
- 1976 Began competing extensively on the East Coast in Black Belt forms, weapons and fighting
- 1976 Began hosting the Top Ten Nationals Karate Championships
- 1976-78 Won 3 out of 4 professional full contact karate matches.
- 1976 Received 1st Degree Black Belt from the National Institute of Martial Arts (NIMA) in a Korean style, Tang Soo Do, Tom Palitini
- 1976 Founded and Documented the American Freestyle Karate System

years of competition and painful experiences, he discovered techniques that were very effective and those which were totally ineffective. Refinement and added techniques have proven over the years to be successful. This system has produced many world champion point, full contact and forms champions for years.

The Black Belt instructors and Masters of American Freestyle Karate are dedicated to the pursuit of excellence in the art. Master Arthur's training methods, motivation, philosophy of instruction, and inspiration have been instilled in his instructors. Master Arthur personally trains each of his Black Belt instructors and teaches them the importance of their task as martial arts instructors.

American Freestyle Karate is like the world we live in. It will continually change in order to adapt itself to new environs, circumstances, technology, and situations. The system will remain on the cutting edge of martial arts instruction and from time to time will lead the way, as history marches on.

PERSONAL & MAJOR ACHIEVEMENTS

- 1978 Received 2nd Degree Black Belt from American Martial Arts Association under Jan Wellendorf (AMAA)
- 1982 Invented and Patented new karate safety equipment, "DURA" Gloves, Boots and Shin Guards. Patent # 4,361,912
- 1982 Article in the 1982 edition of "Who's Who in Martial Arts"
- 1983 Won "Chuck Norris Free for a Day" nationwide contest by Orion Pictures for enrolling the most new students in one month.
- 1986 Established the Super Kicks Karate license program.
- 1986 Founded the American Freestyle Karate Association (AFKA)
- 1986 Licensed first Super Kicks school in Pawtucket, Rhode Island to Grand Master James Perlini.
- 1992 Produced 26 Public Access TV shows, "The Dynamics of American Freestyle Karate". Documenting the AFKA system.
- 1992 Founded the AFKA tournament circuit and promoted the AFKA National Finals.
- 1994 Qualified as a member of the DKT Force One National Karate Team.
- 1995 Won the WKO World Championships, Heavy Weight Fighting Division, held in Port of Spain, Trinidad
- 1995 Named "Top 200 Schools" by Martial Arts Business Magazine Andrew Wood
- 1996 Named "Top 200 Schools" by Martial Arts Business Magazine
- 1997 Named "Top 200 Schools" by Martial Arts Business Magazine
- 1998 Founded and coached Team AFKA National Competition Team
- 2000 Named National Black Belt League (NBL) Arbitrator of the Year
- 2001 Began expansion of the Super Kicks Academies, opened 2nd and 3rd locations
- 2001 Founded the yearly AFKA Hall of Fame
- 2001 Received title of Grand Master from AFKA Master's Council.
- 2002 Opened fourth Academy
- 2002 Named NBL "Man of the Year"

PERSONAL & MAJOR ACHIEVEMENTS

- 2003 Named NBL "Arbitrator of the Year"
- 2003 Awarded 10th Degree Black Belt through the AMAA, by O'Sensei Jan Wellendorf and Hanshi Jessie Bowen
- 2004 Honored as a "Sport Karate Living Legend" by Professor Gary Lee
- 2005 Documented the AFKA Certified Instructor Training Program (CIT)
- 2006 Documented the AFKA Master Instructor Training Program
- 2007 Continued to grow AFKA to 7 Academies, 1,600 members in 5 cities, 3 states.
- 2008 Founded the Independent Black Belt Association, IBBA, a sister organization to the AFKA
- 2010 Grew AFKA to 12 locations
- 2011 Founded the Black Belt Success Systems consulting firm to train martial arts instructors on proper business practices
- 2015 Feature Article as a Legend in the 2015 "Who's Who in Martial Arts".
- 2016 Published 40th Year Anniversary "AFKA BLACK BELT CURRICULUM MANUAL"
- 2016 Feature Article in 2016 "Who's Who in Martial Arts".
- 2017 Will be featured on cover of Martial Arts Success Magazine and to be featured on cover of Tae Kwon Do Times

Bobby S. Briggs

"The Martial Arts has always, and continues to teach me valuable lessons in life."

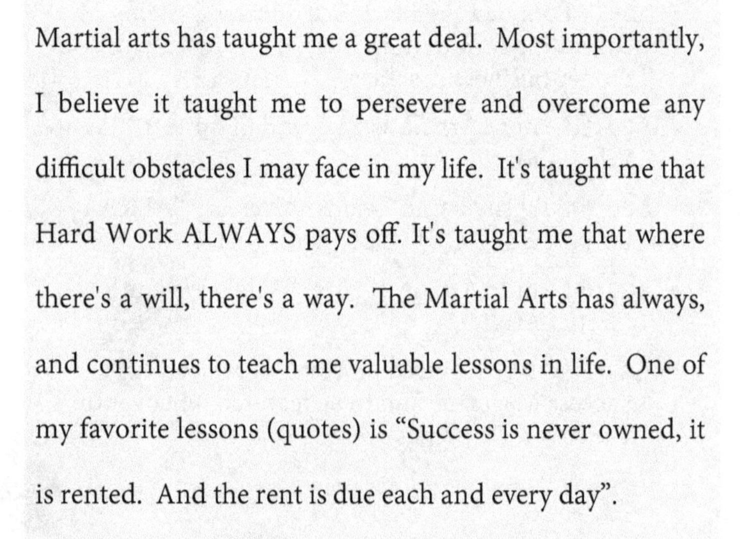

Martial arts has taught me a great deal. Most importantly, I believe it taught me to persevere and overcome any difficult obstacles I may face in my life. It's taught me that Hard Work ALWAYS pays off. It's taught me that where there's a will, there's a way. The Martial Arts has always, and continues to teach me valuable lessons in life. One of my favorite lessons (quotes) is "Success is never owned, it is rented. And the rent is due each and every day".

BIO

As a small poor farm kid, I always had a fascination with the Martial Arts. Mainly because it was something that was so mysterious to me. And I also loved anything physical for as long as I can remember, (like football, boxing, Martial Arts, & etc.). I was a huge Bruce Lee fan, and also became a huge Chuck Norris fan at the same time. I played all kinds of sports all throughout school. I had a boxing coach recommend to me at one time that I should take a Karate class to help with my coordination.

TRAINING INFORMATION

- Martial Arts Styles & Ranks: Kidokime-ryu Karate-do, 10th Degree, JuDan; Okinawa-te, 9th Degree, KuDan; Kenpo Karate, 5th Degree, GoDan; Shotokan, 1st Degree, ShoDan; Shito-ryu, 1st Degree, ShoDan; American Gojo-ryu, 1st Degree, Shodan; Isshin-ryu Karate, 1st Degree; American Karate, 1st Degree, ShoDan; Hapkido, 1st Degree; Tae Kwon Do, 1st Degree
- Instructors/Influencers: Hanshi James White, Hanshi Bill Daniels, Kyoshi David Ray, Kyoshi Rick Sparks, Kyoshi Ken Herfurth, Sensei Chuck Taylor, Sensei Greg McMahan, Sensei Arvin Pearson, Sensei Ernest Watkins, Sensei Ronnie Delfino, Sensei Tony Simmons
- Birthdate: May 24, 1962
- Birthplace/Growing Up: Spruce Pine, NC / Burnsville, NC
- Yrs. In the Martial Arts: 52-53 years
- Yrs. Instructing: 43 years
- School Owner, Manager & Instructor at Kidokime-ryu Karate-do Hombu Dojo, Ranking Black Belt for Kidokime-ryu Karate-do

PROFESSIONAL ORGANIZATIONS

- National Universal Karate Association (N.U.K.A.)
- American Martial Arts Association (AMAA)
- Professional Karate Association (PKA)
- Kenpo Karate Institute (KKI)

Little did he know that I had already gone to some Karate classes as often as my family could afford to let me go. But when my boxing mentor said this to me, I became more serious about the Martial Arts. Since my family could not afford my Karate classes, I worked harder to try and find ways to make money so I could attend Karate classes as often as possible. Since I also loved sports so much, it soon became apparent to me that my Karate was very helpful in me excelling in that also. Karate seemed to enhance my athletic ability in the sports that I played a great deal. But very soon, I found out that as much as I loved sports, Karate very quickly became the love of my life. I never gave up on sports. As a matter of fact, my Karate and the sports that I played throughout school complimented each other very well. The area where I was raised, there were very, very few places where I could go to find a Martial Arts School. Luckily for me, I did find some that had awesome Instructors that led me in the right direction and became a very important figure in my life, and that's where and how my Martial Arts career began.

PERSONAL ACHIEVEMENTS

- Soke Briggs has competed, won, and placed in hundreds of both sport Karate (point fighting, Kata, Weapons, and Self-Defense), as well as, full-contact kickboxing all across the world, and has won numerous times, and defending Champion in many different categories.

MAJOR ACHIEVEMENTS

- Inducted into the Martial Arts Legends Hall of Fame as the Karate Grandmaster of the Year
- Inducted into the Action Martial Arts Hall of Honors/Hall of Heroes for Outstanding Achievements in the Martial Arts as a Grand Master
- Inducted into the Action Martial Arts Magazine World History Book, Action Martial Arts Magazine Hall of Honors,
- Official 20th Anniversary Issue
- AMAA Who's Who in the Martial Arts Hall of Honors
- AMAA Legends Golden Achievement Award (50 Years)
- Numerous Military (both Peacetime and Combat) Awards, Decorations, and Medals
- Numerous Civilian Police Awards and Recognition
- Numerous Civic Awards and Recognitions

Dennis Brown

> "Martial arts has afforded me the opportunity to travel the world. In doing so, I have met so many amazing people..."

Martial Arts makes it possible for me to pursue my dream of helping others to see and experience the benefits of the positive influence and impact that it can have on your life, as it has on mine. I have a wonderful family. Martial arts has afforded me the opportunity to travel the world. In doing so, I have met so many amazing people who continue to share their knowledge, friendship and love. I am blessed and thankful.

BIO

Grand Master Dennis Brown: Fifty-Six Years and Still Training:

The high school that I attended in Washington, D.C. was an exceptional school. It was city champions in football, basketball, baseball and track and field. I was too small for football, too short for basketball, too slow for track, and still can't hit a baseball. I was looking for a sport that would work for me, and so I chose martial arts.

TRAINING INFORMATION

- Martial Arts Styles & Ranks: Tae Kwon Do (1st Degree Black Belt), Tien Shan Pai (Grand Master), Tai Chi Chuan, Chin-Na, Shuai Jiao
- Instructors/Influencers: Shifu Josephus Colvin, Grand Master Jhoon Rhee, Grand Master Willy Lin, Coach Wang Jin Bou
- Birthdate: 1948
- Birthplace/Growing Up: Alexandria, VA / West Virginia & Washington, DC
- Yrs. In the Martial Arts: 56 years
- Yrs. Instructing: 51 years
- School Owner

PROFESSIONAL ORGANIZATIONS

- Chairman, Wang QiHei Taijiquan Association of Hebei, China
- Senior Board of Director, Educational Funding Company, leading business consulting group for martial arts schools
- Senior Board Member, North American Sport Karate Association (NASKA), one of America's oldest martial arts circuits and sanctioning boards

When asked about my martial arts career and how it all began, I have got to admit that it was not a conscious choice or planned desire. I was introduced to the arts in 1965 while attending Howard University. I was living in Drew Hall on campus while awaiting the up-and-coming school year and had heard that there was a karate class going on at the school gym, so I decided to go over to observe what actually turned out to be a Judo class run by an instructor that I believe was named Dr. Yang, who turned out to be Korean. While watching some of the throwing drills, I witnessed one of the students injure his leg when falling. Needless to say, I never went back for a second class and assumed that was not for me – wrong place at the wrong time. But I went on to join the University's Air Force ROTC Drill Team, where my drill sergeant, a gentleman we called "Hook," introduced me to Karate. I immediately realized that I enjoyed kicking a lot more than being thrown and hitting the mat.

And so, it began for me in the basement of a local junior high school across the street from the University, where I discovered a small group of guys training in something called Guo Shu or Kung Fu. It was not the most popular style at the time. In fact, few had ever heard of it -- just a few guys who had ventured into China Towns in D.C. and NY to attend a limited number of classes for foreigners. Gaining the trust and respect of the Shi Fus was difficult for outsiders and in some cases took years.

So, most of my early training was whatever I could pick up from those few students who had ventured into China

PERSONAL ACHIEVEMENTS

- Recognized by Black Belt Magazine as one of the "25 Most Influential Martial Artists of the 20th Century."
- "Only non-Chinese featured in the 1998 Discovery Channel documentary, "The Secrets of the Warrior's Power."
- First African-American martial artist to appear on the covers of Inside Kung-Fu and Kung Fu Tai Chi magazines.
- Master instructor of Tai Chi, Chin-Na and other internal systems
- Redesigned and revolutionized the rope dart, which is arguably the most exotic Chinese weapon to master and he remains one of the few living experts.
- Founder/owner Dennis Brown Shaolin Wu-Shu Centers in Washington, D.C. area
- Wrote, hosted and produced one of the first martial arts talk shows, "Martial Arts Showcase," for Howard University that included special guest interviews and appearances from world renowned martial artists.
- City of Washington, D.C. proclaimed September 11, 1982 as Dennis Brown Day for his ongoing work in the community.

MAJOR ACHIEVEMENTS

- Represented kung fu and wushu in the Wesley Snipes TNT documentary, "A Tribute to the Masters of the Arts."
- Featured in historical documentaries: "The Black Kung Fu Experience," "Urban Dragons," and "How I Made It in America."
- Appeared on the covers of every major national martial arts publication of the last five decades.
- First African-American to train in the People's Republic of China, an historical first.
- Starred in movies in Taiwan, Hong Kong and Bangkok landing the lead role in a major kung fu movie and becoming the only non-Chinese to be directed by legendary Shaw Brothers director Chang Cheh, who started the kung fu movie craze of the 60s.
- June 2017 was honored to be appointed Chairman of the Wan Qihe Taijiquan Association of Hebei Province in the People's Republic of China for the United States, and the only American to represent China's leading style of Tai Chi and meditation in the U.S.

Town and what we could pick up from the Chinese theaters that showed Kung Fu movies from Hong Kong on the weekends. Our classes were mostly held in the city parks or any school gym that would allow us in on the weekend.

After years of moving around to wherever we could find space to train, I decided to attend one of the few formal schools available, Jhoon Rhee's Tae Kwon Do School, where I trained with many of his top black belts that he had brought with him from Texas who later went on to become his world champions. It gave me a foundation that would help me throughout my long career.

My formal training in Kung Fu actually started when I happened to see a small sign in the window of a Tracy's Karate School while driving through town that read," Kung Fu-Tai Chi." I stopped in for information where I met Willy Lin, who would become my Shifu and mentor from then 1971 until now, and allow me a front row seat to the evolution of martial arts in America.

Even though I was still a young kid in the 50s, I remember the martial arts in America was then all about Judo. It was a fighting art that had been brought back to the U.S. by the many soldiers that had been stationed in Japan during war time and were now returning home with these fighting and training skills. In the 60s, things started to change as men were returning from, what would be called the "Korean Conflict," with the Korean fighting arts which would become Tae Kwon Do. The schools were

MAJOR ACHIEVEMENTS

- August 13, 2007, at a simple tea ceremony rarely held in public, Grand Master Willy Line passed along "The Robe and Bowl" of Tien Shan Pai to his disciple of over 40 years, declaring Dennis Brown as Grand Master of the system. He is now officially YiBen, or heir apparent to the world-famous fighting system, which originated in the Tien Shan Pai mountains of northeastern China.
- Promoter of the long-running US Capitol Classics China Open international martial arts competition.
- Certifications from Jiangsu Sport Center in Nanjing and the Beijing Institute of Physical Education
- Inducted into Karate's Black Belt Hall of Fame and Kung Fu's Inside Kung Hall of Fame

BIO (continued)

professionally run and would organize and dominate the times.

But just as many thought there was nothing else new, along came Bruce Lee and David Carradine and Chinese Kung Fu became the rage of the 70s and a new era of flash and excitement was born. No one could have foreseen the arrival of the Ninja Turtles in the 80s as Nin-Jit-Su dominated the martial arts scene and everyone, for the first time, wanted to wear a mask. But in the 90s, who could have predicted that Billy Blanks, a world champion fighter, would launch Tae Bo and no martial arts school would be able to survive without Cardio Kick Boxing.

2000 brought with it the decade of Jiu-Jitsu. Not just Jiu -Jitsu, the Brazilian Jiu-Jitsu. Not just Brazilian, but Gracie Brazilian Jiu-Jitsu, and it was crowned the ultimate system of fighting. 2010 claimed to have brought together the best of all the previous decades of fighting arts, including American Boxing. MMA arrived displaying all of what we have learned.

But, if we have really learned anything, it is that each generation evolves and changes. This is the generation of internal thinking. Wars will include strong minds as well as bodies. My 55+ years of martial arts tells me this 2020 is the decade of the Art of Tai Chi Chuan "The Grand Ultimate Fist," the development of the Mind, Body and Spirit.

David Castro

"I practice what I can, the best I can, and consider all techniques useful in a self-defense situation."

I've come across so many different styles of martial arts. They all have very interesting and valuable techniques to offer. I know I could perfect a few techniques, but it would take another lifetime to perfect or master them all. So, I practice what I can, the best I can, and consider all techniques useful in a self-defense situation. I do know there is no guarantee what I practice will work when I use it because success depends on my opponent's skills, whether there's a weapon involved, the surrounding environment, and my physical condition at that moment. I can only respond, expecting the worst and hoping for the best.

Traditional and non-traditional techniques are all important. Training sharpens my mind and reactionary skills. All of it is very much self-satisfying and useful. Martial arts feed into my everyday life, growth, and development.

TRAINING INFORMATION

- Martial Arts Styles & Ranks: 6th Degree – Matsudaira-ryu Nihon Jujutsu, 6th Degree – Judo, 5th Degree – Ninjitsu Tiger Claw, 4th Degree – Okinawan Goju, 2nd Degree - Taekwondo, studied U.S. Army Combatives; Praying Mantis; Pakua; Dim Mak; Tai Chi; Batto Sword; Budo Tai Jitsu; Jeet Kune Do; Krav Maga; and Black Dragon Fighting Society techniques
- Instructors/Influencers: GM Cho Lin Lo, Sifu Lin Chow, GM Robert Dickey & GM Ronald Hansen, GM Wilfredo Molina, GM Joseph Valentine, GM Gogen Yamaguchi, Sonny Mahai, GM Un Yong Kim
- Birthdate: December 10, 1958
- Birthplace/Growing Up: Manhattan, NY
- Yrs. In the Martial Arts: 51 years
- Yrs. Instructing: 41 years
- School Owner, Manager & Instructor

PROFESSIONAL ORGANIZATIONS

- 1974-1976 - Black Dragon Fighting Society (BDS) (Renewal Pending)
- 1978 – U.S. Combat Martial Arts Association (Life Member)
- 1985 - International Black Belt Unity Program (IBBUP) (Life Member)

BIO

I became interested in martial arts when I was ten years old, but I could not start training until I was 12 years old. I lived in the Bronx, New York, on Vyse Avenue. Across the street, three men were bullying my neighbors; I couldn't tell why. I observed the whole thing while looking out my window located on the third floor. The three guys became violent, and one of the neighbors started defending the rest. He chopped, punched, and kicked. Well, I've never seen that before. As he knocked out one guy with a kick, the other two ran behind a car. He just jumped over the car, kicking one in the face and the other in the stomach. In a few moments, all three guys were knocked out. Police arrived shortly after and arrested the three guys. I was amazed and was anxious to learn.

Martial arts centers were not close by, and it was unsafe for me to walk to a school on my own. So, I started training soon after my family moved to 97th Street in Manhattan. At first, I started learning Taekwondo with GM Sonny Mahai and later Goju with Wildcat Molina. I was glad I studied because when I was 15 years old walking my dog in Central Park, I was approached by three adult men wanting to rob me. I reacted automatically like a martial arts maniac. . I grabbed and twisted the guy's wrist, forcing him to drop the knife; simultaneously, I hooked kicked the guy behind me and knocked him out. As I turned back to the guy with the knife, I threw him to the ground, which knocked him out.

PROFESSIONAL ORGANIZATIONS

- 1985-1992 – Fort Bragg Green Team; Black Belt Team
- 1990-1993 – Professional Karate Commission (PKC)
- 1990-1996 – Amateur Athletic Union (AAU)
- 1991-1995 – Fort Bragg North Carolina, U.S. Olympic Representative
- 1992-1995 - Fort Bragg Taekwondo & Karate Team; Head Coach
- 1993-1995 – National Youth Sport Coaches Association (NYSCA)
- 1997 - International Federation of Ju Jitsuans (IFOJJ) (Renewal Pending)
- 1997 – Federation of United Martial Artists (FUMA) (Life Member)
- 2000 – U.S. Martial Arts Association (USMAA) (Life Member)
- 2000 – U.S. Judo Association (Life Member)
- 2007 - President's Challenge Demonstration Center Examiner; Advocacy Expires 2024
- 2021 – U.S. Martial Arts Federation (Life Member)
- 2021 – U.S. Traditional Kodokan Judo (Life Member)
- 2021 – U.S. Ju-Jitsu Federation (Life Member)

PERSONAL ACHIEVEMENTS

- July 2015, Aug 2013 & May 2012 – Presidential Champion – Silver Award (Jiujitsu); from POTUS Barack Obama
- May 2015, July 2013 & Mar 2012 – Presidential Champion – Bronze Award (Jiujitsu); from POTUS Barack Obama
- Apr 2015 & June 2013 – Presidential Champion – Platinum Award (Jiujitsu); from POTUS Barack Obama
- Aug 2011, June 2011, May 2011, Jan 2011, Oct 2010, Jun 2010 & Mar 2010 - National Physical Fitness Award (Jiujitsu); from POTUS Barack Obama
- Aug 2011, June 2011, Mar 2011, Jan 2011, Oct 2010, Aug 2010, Jun 2010 & Mar 2010 – Presidential Active Lifestyle Award (Jiujitsu); from POTUS Barack Obama
- Jun 2011, Mar 2011, Jan 2011, Oct 2010, Aug 2010, Jun 2010 & Mar 2010 – Presidential Physical Fitness Award (Jiujitsu); from POTUS Barack Obama

The third guy ran away. A police officer saw the entire incident; he had me wait for two other police officers to escort me home as he cuffed and arrested the two guys on the ground.

In another situation, at age 16, I was walking a girl home after a movie date. At the entrance of the projects, her ex-boyfriend with a few friends was waiting to start trouble. I told the girl to go home and not to worry, but I was actually scared. Her ex-boyfriend yelled at me, but when two of his friends approached, I threw one punch, and the guy went down, and the other I kicked. Everyone on site must have been confused while watching because I had time to just run home. To avoid more trouble, I never saw the girl again.

As I turned 24, while in the military, I started getting snobby and thought I was a bad dude. So, I decided I would go to a bikers bar in Fayetteville, North Carolina, which did not work out as I planned. I started a fight with one guy, but everyone jumped in, and I ended up getting hit with pool sticks, chairs, mugs, bottles, fists, and boots. They threw me out the rear exit of the place. I woke up calling a taxi cab and went right to the hospital. That was my first and last time doing that. I learned about controlling my attitude, knowing my environment, and improving my self-discipline in the near future.

I had lost myself. You see, I didn't learn martial arts to become a champion, a fighter, or for fame and fortune. I just enjoyed what I learned. As a matter of fact, when I

PERSONAL ACHIEVEMENTS

- Aug 2003 - USMAA Hall of Fame; Law Enforcement Instructor of the Year
- Aug 2002 – USMAA Hall of Fame; Master Instructor of the Year
- Feb 1998 – Letter of Congratulations (Jiujitsu); from PCPFS Co-Chairperson Griffith Joyner
- Feb 1998, Oct 1997, May 1997, Nov 1996, June 1996 & Sep1993 – Presidential Sports Award (Jiujitsu); from POTUS Bill Clinton
- Apr 1995 – DCA Sports Manager; Special Recognition; Head Coach Post Karate Team
- Mar 1994 – Letter of Congratulations (Jiujitsu); from PCPFS Co-Chairperson Griffith Joyner
- Mar 1994 – Letter of Congratulations (Jiujitsu); from PCPFS Chairman Arnold Schwarzenegger
- Feb 1993 - Presidential Sports Award (Jiujitsu); from President George Bush
- Aug 1989 - Presidential Sports Award (Jiujitsu); from President George Bush
- May 1989 – Letter of Congratulations (Jiujitsu); from PCPFS Chairman Richard Kazmaier

started teaching, I never charged my students for lessons. To include, while in the U.S. Army, I borrowed use of local centers on base to teach without charging a fee. Students only needed to buy their uniforms and pay promotion fees. I assessed students to ensure they wanted to learn for the right reasons. My students are never encouraged to compete except for the post karate team. And I always redirect students to other teachers if they want to compete for money (i.e., MMA, UFC, K1, etc.). I always advised to expect to pay for such training, sign contracts, waivers, and non-disclosure agreements. Ensure to have a lawyer review the contracts before signing and be careful.

PERSONAL ACHIEVEMENTS

- Apr 1989, Jan 1989, Oct 1988, July 1988, May 1988 & Mar 1988 - Presidential Sports Award (Jiujitsu); from President George Bush
- Mar 1988 – Letter of Congratulations (Jiujitsu); from PCPFS Chairman Richard Kazmaier
- Jun 1987 - Presidential Sports Award (Jiujitsu); from President Ronald Reagan

MAJOR ACHIEVEMENTS

- Teaching and promoting martial arts for all styles and systems
- July 1977-Jan 2021 – Received multiple Presidential and military service awards associated with teaching martial arts to federal agents, law enforcement, servicemen and women
- 1977-1998 - Tenure in military service provided opportunities to train Military Police, Special Forces, Counterintelligence/Counterterrorism Agents, Law Enforcement Officers, Federal Officials, military Soldiers and Officers, and self-defense to dependent civilians
- 1974-1976 – Rice High School, New York, Martial Arts Club (President & VP)

Joe Ciccone

"I have learned to take whatever works from everything I have been taught and apply it to what is useful."

Martial arts has had a significant impact on my life. When I was a child and was being bullied, it gave me confidence in myself. It has strengthened my body as well as my mind and given me a purpose at times when I felt like I was defeated. Through the many styles I have learned, it was so interesting how different they were yet how intricately woven they could be. How accepting over the years they have become and are more tolerant of other styles. In the early years, it was always a power struggle over which style was the best. There would be a student who excelled in each of these styles, and when they won, they would claim that their style was superior to the others. They couldn't grasp that it was the individual and not so much the training in the art that they represented. I know, through my studies, I have learned to take whatever works from everything I have been taught and apply it to what is useful. When I teach, I recognize not everyone is the same, so, I can specialize in training that

TRAINING INFORMATION

- Martial Arts Styles & Ranks: Sil-lum Kung-Fu 3rd degree black, Wing Chun, Choy le Fut advanced student, Jiu jitsu purple belt, Taekwondo, Tang Soo do 1st Dan, Hapkido
- Instructors/Influencers: Si gong Tai Chueng Sau, Master Duncan Leong, Master Soo Wong Lee, Master Jung Bai Lee, Master Harold Hankins, Master Gary Daniels
- Birthdate: November 20, 1955
- Birthplace/Growing Up: Norfolk, VA / Virginia Beach, VA
- Yrs. In the Martial Arts: 55 years
- Yrs. Instructing: 51 years
- School Owner & Instructor at Yee Chi Kwan Fighting Academy, Founder of Yee chi Kwan

PROFESSIONAL ORGANIZATIONS

- International Federation of Martial Arts
- EUSAIMAA
- International Martial Arts Association

will work for each unique individual. Martial arts has taught me to be resilient in my approach to having a personal impact on my students. When I promote, I use different ways of stimulating my students' achievements, whether it's rewarding them with belts, patches, sashes or certificates. As long as they feel a sense of accomplishment, they will strive to keep learning. I have learned this through many teachers and how their style differs from others. Over the years, I have attained wisdom and knowledge and a proper way of treating people like we need to be treated. If we put people first, we will be able to teach more effectively because people know whether or not you care. If they know you care, it will inspire them to care about others, and they will be better students, teachers, and people in the Martial Arts and in life as a result. Studying Martial Arts has truly impacted my life as well as my students and the people I have come into contact with. I hope people's lives are changed and touched for the best by being a small part of a life that I have tried to live as an example.

BIO

Growing up, I attended a private school until the fifth grade, when I was transferred to a public school. That was an eye opener. In private school, we were like a family, but when it came to public school, that's when the bullying started. I was chubby and dressed conservative, wearing wing tip shoes, an insurance man's briefcase, with Vitalis in my hair. I was begging for a beat down and I didn't even know it. There was one big kid who didn't like my

PERSONAL ACHIEVEMENTS

- TRIS Tidewater Rape Information Services hired me to teach self-defense, and I was an advocate for women's self-defense and training. I was the first person in the state of Virginia to teach and recognize nunchaku as a weapon and get it passed into law, as well as helping develop a side-handled baton modeled after the tonfa. Special Forces specialized training was taught, as well as government agencies specialized training.

MAJOR ACHIEVEMENTS

- Founder and developer of my own style Yee chi Kwan. Competed in full contact free style and won the World Championship in 1975, When it was disbanded in 1978, I was undefeated. I was inducted into the Who's Who of the Martial Arts Elite in 1988 and I was inducted into the Who's Who of the Martial Arts in Karate International in 1992.

face because he was always talking about smashing it in. Every day after class he would beat me down to the ground until finally one day my mother walked into my bedroom when I was changing and saw the bruises all over my body. I had to come clean about the bullying and my mother put a stop to it. A teacher was fired over it because he allowed it to go on. Back in the early sixties, nobody ever did anything about bullying. They never thought it was a big deal. My father introduced me to working out, wrestling, boxing, and martial arts. It was through the Martial Arts that I learned confidence and self-esteem. I became very proficient at fighting and was able to protect myself and others. I would not tolerate bullying by anyone and was quick to come to their defense. As I continued through school, I had many opportunities to face my fears and to become an overcomer. It was the discipline of martial arts, as well as having great teachers in each style I studied, that influenced my life. I sit back and reminisce about my 52 years and realize how fortunate and blessed I've been. The wisdom I have attained through martial arts and my faith in God has changed the direction of my life for the better. I can only hope to continue on the path set before me, to give to others the knowledge and faith that I have learned.

John Chung

"Martial Arts has taught me to see, experience and live life positively and gratefully."

BIO

At a young age, I was interested in the Martial Arts. In Korea, I took Judo at my Middle School. In 1970, at the age of 12, I came to Washington, D.C and began my training in Tae Kwon Do with my Uncle, Founding Father of American Tae Kwon Do Grand Master Jhoon Rhee. Martial Arts has taught me to be a student for and of life. It has taught me the benefits of being a competitor and the joy of being the best individual that I choose to be.

The passion of Martial Arts has given me the opportunity to pay it forward by teaching since 1972. I have also been Blessed as a competitor, to be the Champion of the World, and to have traveled and enjoyed many Martial Artists and their cultures from various countries.

My philosophy: Learn Something, Get a Good workout and Have Fun! This has been my school motto and theme where students of all ages benefit.

TRAINING INFORMATION

- Martial Arts Title: World Forms & Fighting Champion
- Reston, VA
- Started Studying Martial Arts in 1970
- Instructing Martial Arts for 45 years and currently holds the rank of 9th Dan Black Belt studying martial arts styles: Tae Kwon Do
- Instructor: Grand Master Jhoon Rhee

PERSONAL ACHIEVEMENTS

- 1976, Graduated Wakefield High School, Arlington, Virginia
- 1984, Wake Forest University, B.S. in Business Administration, Winston-Salem, North Carolina

Martial Arts has taught me to see, experience and live life positively and gratefully. I believe the president of 1st grade is just as important as a person as the president of a company. Everyone is treated with respect.

Always try your best, effort is the most important quality and seek joy in your goals and achievements.

Seminars and training camps for Martial Artists of all styles and levels have brought me great opportunities to continually share my experiences as a student, competitor, instructor and business owner. Hosting tournaments and motivational speeches have been well received and appreciated by both Martial Artists and Non -Martial Artists.

In the years 1970-1987, I was fortunate to have competed in all major tournaments, National and Internationally, Winning World Championship titles since 1981. Most Recent Awards: 2014- Masters Hall of Fame, 2014-World Wide Tae Kwon Do Award, 2015-AmeriKick Internationals Hall of Fame, 2016- Joe Lewis Eternal Warrior Award, And . . . 30 years of teaching Boot Camp for Martial Artists. Students from all over the world come to train together to improve, learn and experience world class training.

"People go to camps to meet a Champion. We come to John Chung's camp to become a Champion!"

HIGHLIGHTS:

"The best in the world! "King of Kata!" "World Forms &

PERSONAL TIMELINE:

- 1970: No Belt
- 1974: Black Belt
- 1977: PKA National Champion
- 1979: US Champion
- 1981: World Champion
- 1982: Black Belt Hall of Fame
- 1982: PKA Tournament Competitor of the Year
- 1983: World Champion
- 1984: Inductee Karate Hall of Fame
- 1985: World Champion
- 1989: Diamond Nationals Hall of Fame
- 1990: NASKA Hall of Fame
- 1990: Fighter International Hall of Fame
- 1993: World Martial Arts Hall of Fame
- 1996: Bluegrass Nationals Hall of Fame
- 1997: Founder of Sidekick International Competition Team
- 1998: Promoter of the Sidekick International Martial Arts Championship
- 1999: Promoter of the World Cup Finals Open Martial Arts Championship
- 2000: President of the World Cup Martial Arts Organization
- 2005: Ocean State Grand Nationals Hall of Fame
- 2006: World Mundo Federation Hall of Fame
- 2009: Universal Martial Arts Association International Hall of Fame
- 2012: All Pro Tae Kwon Do Martial Arts Hall of Fame
- 2013: New York Tournaments Martial Arts Hall of Fame

Fighting champion!" Any describe only one person.

Student of Grandmaster Jhoon Rhee, father of American Tae Kwon Do, John Chung.

John Chung, with his famous perfect side kick and techniques, has revolutionized the level of competition. Pioneer of musical forms and perfectionist of traditional forms, the King of Kata, John Chung, has brought the standard of excellence to the forefront.

World forms & fighting John Chung is passing down his experience and spreading his knowledge of martial arts, to students of Karate, Kung Fu and Tae Kwon Do. The best in the world, John Chung, excels as an instructor. The knowledge to understand and improve technically along with the edge to win in competition is currently given in worldwide seminars. All seminars vary from Tae Kwon Do history, traditional forms, musical forms, self-defense (applications of techniques) to necessary basics in stretching, strengthening, tournament & continuous sparring and open competition.

Bill Clark

"Grand Master Clark has Walked the Talk of EXCELLENCE within the Martial Arts."

BIO

Master Bill Clark became 9th Degree Grand Master William Clark in June, 2016, some five decades after his martial arts journey began. In a moving and spectacular presentation in Little Rock at the ATA World Championship, the organization and its leaders and members showed their appreciation for his lifetime of dedication with the highest rank bestowed on its Masters. In this nearly five-decade journey, Master Clark has touched hundreds of thousands of lives, from students to Chief Masters to friends and associates around the globe.

The new Grand Master Clark began his martial arts saga in 1966 in Omaha, Nebraska. He joined Eternal Grand Master H.U. Lee's first martial arts school in 1968 in the first steps of his life and industry changing voyage.

After achieving second degree black belt rank, with the

TRAINING INFORMATION

- Belt Rank/Titles: 9th Degree Grand Master
- Instructors/Influencers: Eternal Grand Master H.U. Lee
- Birthplace/Growing Up: Jacksonville, FL
- Yrs. In the Martial Arts: 52 years

FROM WHITE BELT TO GRAND MASTER:

Grand Master Clark was born in Jacksonville, Florida where he grew up. He later moved to Omaha, NE to work with his uncle.

- 1966: He started his Martial Arts training in Omaha, Nebraska studying Aikido
- 1968: Trained with Eternal Grand Master HU Lee at Midwest Karate Federation (later known as ATA). During this time, he met and trained with lifelong friends Grand Master Richard Reed and Grand Master Robert Allimeir.
- 1970s: During this decade Master Clark was an integral part of the foundation of the ATA, helping organize & standardize ATA tournaments, helping write the original curriculum instructor's manual and the Scrolls of Songahm (describes the essence and tradition of the martial art). Ranked 8th in SEKA, KI, PKA
- 1971: After receiving the rank of 2nd Degree Black Belt Grand Master Clark headed back home to Jacksonville, Florida to open his first school. It consisted of 900 square feet, no bigger than a two-car garage.

urging and support of Master Lee, Bill Clark opened his first academy in Jacksonville, Florida in 1971. His work ethic, mixed with an exceptional fighter's heart, a quick wit and a sense of loyalty second-to-none, paved the path for success in his first school.

In an expedition that has included world class everything—point fighting, kickboxing, teaching, staff development, management, television commentary, judging, refereeing, seminars, organizing and so much more—Grand Master Clark has Walked the Talk of EXCELLENCE.

FROM WHITE BELT TO GRAND MASTER:

- 1972: After only one year and testing 740 students, Master Clark had to relocate the facility to a stand-alone structure with two training floors, saunas, fitness equipment and offices.
- 1974: Master Clark was awarded ATA Instructor of the year. He also helped set up the ATA Top 10 structure for tournaments and new rules for competition.
- 1976: In addition to his many accomplishments with the ATA that year, Master Clark was an avid fighter in the PKA (Professional Karate Association) and was awarded the PKA fighter of the year award.
- 1978: He officially retired from the tournament circuit after winning the PKA Championships and the ATA Grand National Title
- 1980s: While on the Founders Council of the ATA, helped Eternal Grand Master H.U. Lee create the new Songahm forms with Master Allimeir and Master G.H. Lee
- 1982: Master Clark opened his 2nd and 3rd schools in Jacksonville, to continue the growth of the ATA. Eternal Grand Master H.U. Lee awarded him the Presidential Achievement Award
- 1990s: Master Clark focused on program development for the ATA, helping to bring in weapons training and the Black Belt Club program. He designed and implemented sales procedures for the martial arts industry and became perhaps the most sought after speaker at yearly events such as the Martial Arts Industry Association Supershow, National Association of Professional Martial Artists (NAPMA) convention and others.
- 1997: Received Battle of Atlanta Centurion Award
- 2000s: Master Clark introduced a number of new martial arts styles to the ATA, creating programs that integrated Krav Maga, Kali and street self-defense into the current training.
- 2012: Master Clark was inducted into the International Martial Arts Hall of Fame.
- 2013: Received the Joe Lewis Eternal Warrior Award
- 2013: Received the Martial Arts Industry Association's Lifetime Achievement Award for his dedication to the martial arts.
- 2015: Earned the rank of Grand Master 9th degree Black Belt with the World Black Belt Association.
- 2016: Earns Grand Master Rank alongside lifelong friend Rob Allemeier.

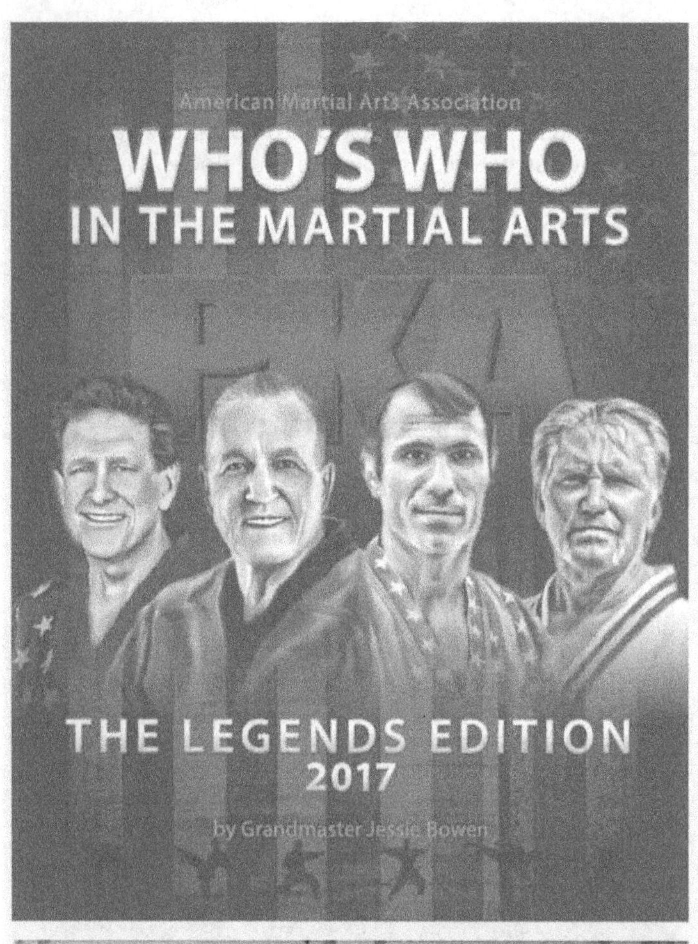

FROM WHITE BELT TO GRAND MASTER:

- 2016: GM Clark wrote and filmed the first PERSONAL GROWTH program for Martial Artists. GM Clark continues to be focused on real-life Leadership Development, to ensure Eternal Grand Master H.U. Lee's vision is faithfully carried into the future.
- 2017: Featured on the cover of Who's Who Legends with lifelong friends Bill Wallace, Jeff Smith and Joe Corley
- 2018-19: The introduction of the new global website TheEvolutionofKrav.com to augment the incredibly well organized Warrior Krav Maga System. Check it Out!

Reggie Cochran

Dr. Reggie Cochran, PhD, DCH (Doctor of Clinical Hypnotherapy) is a consultant and business partner with GM Norris and his wife Gena. Reggie is an internationally known Consultant, Coach, Speaker, Best Selling Author & Cross Disciplined Champion Martial Artist.

Reg has co-authored books with Bill Gates, Donald Trump, Brian Tracy, Dr. Wayne Dyer, Deepak Chopra, to name a few. The latest book he coauthored "Think and Grow Rich Today hit #1 Best Seller status on Amazon the first day it was released. This earned him the coveted Quilly Award and induction into the National Academy of Best Selling Authors.

His personal clients read like an international who's who directory filled with actors, entertainers, pro wrestlers, MMA champs, Gold & Platinum recording artist / musicians, top 1% entrepreneurs and business professionals.

Dr. Reg is an Independent Strategic Intervention Coach. Reggie received his Strategic Intervention Coach training from the prestigious Robbins-Madanes Center, founded by Tony Robbins and Cloe Madanes. Reg is also an Independent Certified Coach, Teacher and Speaker with The John Maxwell Team.

His coaching, speaking. and writing has earned him 3 EXPY awards. This keeps him in high demand as a keynote speaker and trainer for audiences ranging from youth to corporate events.

Reggie found discipline and direction in the martial arts after his father passed away. He feels fortunate to have been able to train with some very talented instructors, to train with others that challenged him to become better, and to get to know many people around the world, that have become close family, friends, mentors and role models to him.

His martial arts career has many facets. As a martial arts competitor he has won many state, national, international and World Champion titles. He opened his first martial arts studio in 1978 and has been blessed to have helped thousands of students over the decades. Now most of his time in the martial arts world is spent serving his martial arts brothers and sisters through the various Board positions he has.

Due to his father's suicide, today he is working on a complete online training series geared to help people recover from various types of surgeries, injuries, and PTSD. He is very passionate on this as his dad took his life due to PTSD from a severe war injury.

He's a long-time member of the United Fighting Arts Federation and has earned a 9th Degree Black Belt from his instructor, GM Chuck Norris. Reggie has served in various UFAF leadership positions since 1986. He is currently on the UFAF Board of Directors UFAF BJJ and special projects.

Sensei Reg is also a 10th degree Black Belt awarded by GM Pat Burleson, GM Ted Gambordello and recognized by the Professional Karate Association Board of Directors lead by GM Joe Corley, GM Jeff Smith & GM Bill Wallace. Today Reg also serves on the Board of Directors for the PKA.

Professor Reg earned a 2nd Degree Black Belt in Brazilian Jiu Jitsu from Professors Richard Norton, David Dunn, Chuck Norris & Rickson Gracie.

Sifu Reg also holds Master Instructor ranks in Kung Fu, Tai Chi and Qui Gong and is a Director for the International Chinese Boxing Association.

He is also a cofounding member of the International Federation of Mixed Martial Artist with Big John McCarthy and David Dunn. The IFMMA was one of the first organizations to offer a structured training and ranking program in MMA.

He is a multi-time martial arts Hall Of Fame member, Chuck Norris Man of The Year, recipient of the first Howard Jackson Memorial Award, The Sport Karate Museum Chuck Norris Natural Fighter award, Joe Lewis Eternal Warrior award and the UFAF Wieland Norris award.

Although Dr. Reg is very humbled and proud of his various martial arts accomplishments, titles and ranks, he also understands that with those things, comes much greater responsibility of serving others, not being served. He does not like to be called Master, Grand Master etc. as he still considers himself a work in progress and a life-long student.

As an instructor, his goals have always been to help each student become much better and successful than he has been. Most importantly he trains his students to take the discipline and focus they learn in the studio and apply to the rest of their personal and business lives.

Reggie will be the first to tell you that most of his accomplishments as a speaker, author and coach are partially due to the skills he learned from his martial arts instructors GM Chuck Norris, GM Richard Norton, GM Al Francis, GM Ted Gambordello & Professor David Dunn.

He also credits his success to every person he fought in the ring and trained in seminars with over the decades. Each match and each seminar reinforced and layered his determination, discipline and focus to be the best he can be in all areas of his life.

But first and foremost, he gives credit to God and his Lord and Savior Jesus Christ. Second to his wife Thresa Cochran who has stood by his side to support and encourage him. Thresa is also has Black Belts from GM Chuck Norris and GM Al Francis. And taught beside Reg over the years.

When asked what his highest titles are, his response is normally husband, father and grandpa. He continually strives to be a positive role model and influence to his family and friends. And to spread the good news of God's love, forgiveness and healing power through Jesus, with as many people as possible.

Joe Corley

"Martial Arts provided me with the opportunity to learn so many skills that apply to so many aspects of life."

BIO

Atlanta's Joe Corley is still a black belt and sports entrepreneur with a mission, most recently honored for Lifetime Achievement in the 2019 Who's Who in Martial Arts and on the cover of the 2017 LEGENDS edition of the AMAA Who's Who in the Martial Arts 2017 edition. Now a Grand Master instructor with more than 5 decades experience in the martial arts, and the producer of PKA KARATE & KICKBOXING for television, Corley's life-long purpose for being has been to share with everyone the positive feelings of confidence, courage, intensity, focus, personal discipline and integrity engendered by good martial arts training and competition. He has done that through the promotion of the martial arts in his Atlanta chain of studios, through his Battle of Atlanta World Karate Championship and on television around the world.

Corley began his karate classes at age 16, earned his black belt at 19, opened his first studio at 19, won three US titles in the next three years, founded the Battle of Atlanta at age 23 and has fervently spread the word ever since. Joe has sought to share the most practical physical karate movements available and combine those real-life defensive techniques with modern American positive philosophy.

There are but a handful of men in the martial arts anywhere in the world who have accomplished so much for the furtherance of the martial arts philosophy and physical applications. As a fighter, Joe Corley won three United States Championships in point karate and went on to retire as the number one ranked Middle Weight contender in the world. Now a 10th degree Black Belt in American Karate, Mr. Corley and his Black Belts have taught more than 50,000 men, women and children in his chain of Atlanta studios.

As a Black Belt in Tang Soo Do, he opened Atlanta's first full time karate studio in 1967 while he was still competing and expanded the studios to become the most well-known martial arts chain in the Southeast.

In 1970, Joe Corley founded the BATTLE OF ATLANTA, one of the most prestigious open karate tournaments in the world. The Battle of Atlanta recently completed its Golden Anniversary and the GATHERING OF WORLD CHANGERS. The Battle, now owned and produced by Truth Entertainment, again hosted competitors from all

HUMILITY OF A GRANDMASTER 10TH DEGREE CERTIFICATE

One who has achieved the rank of GRAND MASTER in MARTIAL ARTS, in fact,

DOES NOT FEEL WORTHY…

Having BATTLED through the WARRIOR BLACK BELT RANKS OF 1ST, 2ND and 3RD DEGREE

And Having PROUDLY ADMINISTERED the TEACHER / INSTRUCTOR RANKS OF 4TH and 5th DEGREE

And Having SKILLFULLY & MASTERFULLY

EDUCATED THE INSTRUCTORS as a PROFESSOR 6th and 7th DEGREE and

Having CONSISTENTLY and DUTIFULLY GIVEN BACK TO THE MARTIAL ARTS COMMUNITY as 8TH and 9th DEGREE

The GRANDMASTER knows what he does not know; he knows how much there is left to learn.

At the same time, he embodies the sentiments in Master Educator Stephen R. Covey's 7 HABITS and his expression of HUMILITY: "Humility is the mother of all virtues. Courage is the father. Integrity the Child. Wisdom the Grandchild."

Having honorably carried out the BLACK BELT RESPONSIBILITIES above and having demonstrated exceptionally the virtues of

WISDOM, INTEGRITY, COURAGE and HUMILITY

THE PROFESSIONAL KARATE COMMISSION

DOES HEREBY BESTOW UPON

JOE CORLEY

THE GRAND MASTER RANK OF

10th DEGREE BLACK BELT

over the world. In this same period, Art Heller joined Joe Corley, Sam Chapman, Bill McDoanald, Larry Reinhardt and Jack Motley in a meeting with Chuck Norris to kick off the South East karate Association (SEKA) from which so many great Southeast Champions emerged.

In 1975, Joe Corley challenged Bill "Superfoot" Wallace for his PKA World Middleweight Title in what became a historic fight before 12,000 fans in Atlanta's Omni. Wallace won the first of its kind 9 round bout. Master Corley would later be hired by CBS to cover Superfoot's future bouts because of his ability to articulate the inner workings of the sport and the techniques and strategies of the fighters.

Because of the great ratings at CBS, Master Corley also became the voice for American Karate and PKA KICKBOXING on other networks. He actually produced the programming and did commentary with long-term friends like Chuck Norris and the late Pat Morita (Mr. Miyagi) on NBC, CBS, ESPN, SHOWTIME, USA NETWORK, TURNER SPORTS, SPORTSCHANNEL AMERICA, PRIME NETWORK, SPORTSOUTH

and on international television syndication. As expert analyst and host for PKA KARATE World Championships on network, cable and pay per view, Mr. Corley became synonymous with the sport to the millions of fans who followed the 1,000+ hours of coverage on television.

BIO (continued)

With events originating from such diverse locales as Canada, France, Belgium, South Africa, South America and the United Arab Emirates plus 50 cities in the United States, Joe Corley has educated 4 generations of sports fans.

Master Corley has been named Official Karate Magazine's Man of the Decade, was inducted into the prestigious Black Belt Magazine Hall of Fame and the International Tae Kwon Do Hall of Fame and has received more awards than anyone can count.

But the thing that continues to drive Joe Corley is the knowledge that he and his accomplished associates can use all their experiences to share with everyone around the world on television the great feelings of confidence, courage, discipline, honor and integrity that come from presenting the martial arts properly. His PKA WORLDWIDE KICKBOXING projects are the perfect vehicles to spread the messages of positive martial arts on a global scale.

"The unequalled success of the UFC, built on our previous successes, has set the stage for PKA Fighters to achieve the 'fame and fortune' the athletes of the UFC are now enjoying", he said.

Joe is in regular meetings with astute sports entrepreneurs in order to kick off the new project for 2020 and beyond. "We have the UFC's own research to indicate the timing is perfect for us now", he said. At the same time, he is building the grass roots for PKA WORLDWIDE Associated Schools and Members, bringing together the best martial artists from around the globe.

Mr. Corley's bride--Christina-- is his right arm and chief administrator in PKA WORLDWIDE. Mr. Corley's daughter, Christiana, 22, continues to be his lustrous link in this new millennium and his compelling force to make the martial arts world an even better place.

Master Corley's closest friends point to the PKC 10th Degree Grand Master certificate, saying the language of the certificate reflects the philosophy and humility they know to be the real Joe Corley (See above).

Master Corley is consulting with a number of martial artists to share his experience and wisdom and has been recruited to consult on other projects outside the martial arts. One such project is the introduction of a generation system destined to change the worlds of Solar, Wind Generation and Electric Vehicles.

"Martial arts provided me with the opportunity to learn so many skills that apply to so many aspects of life", he said. "I look forward to this 'next half' of my time on the planet applying the skills learned. I also fiercely love being a student, and I look forward to learning as much as I can in this last half. Learning brings me joy", he smiled.

"After 19 years as a 9th Degree Black Belt, I was so proud to earn my 10th Degree from the PKC and Grand Master

Grand Master's Jeff Smith & Joe Corley receive their PKC 10th Degree Black Belts at Battle of Atlanta 2016

Glenn Keeney in 2016. I was honored to have GM Pat Johnson, GM Allen Steen and GM Pat Burleson approve the PKC promotion. It was doubly sweet because lifelong friend Jeff Smith earned his that same day. These 5 men have all had such a great influence on my martial arts career in so many ways, and it was so very special to share the experience with all of them!"

John Cox

"Molding an individual to be what they want to become is unbelievably rewarding."

How has studying the Martial Arts impacted my life? Wow, that's an easy question with a not so easy answer. Responsibility, discipline, accountability, drive. Next, humility, the drive to teach others, gratitude for what you have/earned, and hope for a better future for all. My joy comes from teaching others, helping them achieve their goals and dreams. Molding an individual to be what they want to become is unbelievably rewarding. To be blessed with achieving my goals in life is beyond words. Knowing I have the drive and the will to keep achieving new goals has a calming effect on me.

BIO

I first became interested in martial arts when I was 8 or 9 years old, after watching wrestling on TV with a friend who had some martial arts magazines. I started playing around with a friend who had some basic training in Kung fu, tiger style, I believe. Another school friend told me about a guy teaching Kung fu, wing Chun to be exact.

TRAINING INFORMATION

- Martial Arts Styles & Ranks: Kidokime-ryu Karate-do, 10th Degree, JuDan; Okinawa-te, 9th Degree, KuDan; Kenpo Karate, 5th Degree, GoDan; Shotokan, 1st Degree, ShoDan; Shito-ryu, 1st Degree, ShoDan; American Gojo-ryu, 1st Degree, Shodan; Isshin-ryu Karate, 1st Degree; American Karate, 1st Degree, ShoDan; Hapkido, 1st Degree; Tae Kwon Do, 1st Degree
- Instructors/Influencers: Michael Green, Garrison Hall, Al Tracy, Oshiro Mizuno, Hamiko Nishimoto
- Birthdate: September 16, 1960
- Birthplace/Growing Up: Greenville, SC
- Yrs. In the Martial Arts: 51 years
- Yrs. Instructing: 46 years
- School Owner, Manager & Instructor at Haigashi Sai Self Defense Systems

PROFESSIONAL ORGANIZATIONS

- International Martial Arts Society
- International Board of Black Belts - World Black Belt Council
- International Combat M.A. Unions Association
- United States Martial Artist Association

Fast forward: I persuaded my mother to meet him, and they agreed to let me start taking lessons on the condition that I not tell anyone. Mom was afraid I'd get into fights or be bullied into fights, so I kept it to myself and my kwoon mates. My early beginnings were triggered by a Bruce Tenner book, which I still have, and training was extremely difficult, monotonous, and fascinating. Wing Chun was a single-family style from China that evolved into the Na. That is where I stayed, and eventually I inherited that system.

PERSONAL ACHIEVEMENTS

- 30-year career firefighter, retired
- State licensed residential builder
- NRA firearms Instructor
- America in Defense flight crew instructor
- International accredited fire instructor
- Martial Arts Instructor for 46 years

MAJOR ACHIEVEMENTS

- Action Martial Arts Magazine H.O.F. Inductee 3 times
- London International M.A. H.O.F. Inductee
- Universal M.A. Association H.O.F. Inductee
- Action M.A. Radio H.O.F. Inductee
- Black Warrior M.A. H.O.F. Inductee
- Martial Arts Masters and Pioneers book inclusion (three times)
- Action Martial Arts Magazine Hall of Honors book inclusion (twice)

Al Dacascos AKA Sifual

Professional maximizer, martialologist, life coach, Stunt/Fight Choreographer/ Producer, author, and father of Mark Dacascos, an actor, director, martial artist, and television personality.

Since the founding of his unique fighting art, Wun Hop Kuen Do, in 1969, Al Dacascos has become one of our era's most noted martial artists. A 9th Degree black belt, Dacascos has won over 200 championships and appeared on just as many martial arts magazine covers over the years. 1969 to 1973, he was listed as one of the top 10 fighters in America and Number 1 in the Rocky Mountain region according to Professional Karate and Black Belt magazines. In 1975, Mr. Dacascos was invited to appear in ABC's Wide World of Sports in Los Angeles. He gave a breathtaking demonstration so impressed with WHKD that a German delegation offered Dacascos the opportunity to expand his schools and give seminars throughout Europe. In 1977, he was inducted into the Black Belt Hall of Fame as Instructor of the Year and again in 1992 by Inside Kung Fu Magazine. Charter member of the Martial Arts History Museum Hall of Fame, Dacascos was voted into the first class in 1999 with martial arts luminaries including Bruce Lee, Benny Urquidez (aka The Jet), Chuck Norris, Toshirô Mifune, and Cynthia Rothrock. Dacascos had more votes than Norris, Mifune, and Rothrock. As a visionary and innovator, he has manifested the dream of creating a network of schools, five generations strong of black belts to reflect his style. He authored

"Legacy, through the Eyes of a Warrior." A 5 Star Amazon Book and top seller, 2016.

Concurrently, working with his partner Sean Harflinger, developing movie projects for their company Funky Puppy Production LLC., DTS (Dacascos Technical Systems), an innovative and different approach to personal protection and co-promoting and hosting "The Ultimate Warriors Cup Championships" with SGM Ron Van Clief.

James Debrow

"Karate has been my life and still is today...Martial Arts is the best thing that ever happened to me!"

Martial arts have added value to my life and gave me the following skills: discipline, respect, motivation, trust, leadership, communication, teamwork, teaching, follower, emotional control, physical fitness, mental fitness, resiliency, character, spirituality, attention span growth, calmness, loyalty, commitment, veracity, tenacity, competitiveness, goal orientation, cognition, and motor performance.

Martial arts helped me to meet all races, both male and female domestic and international. I worked with elementary, junior high school, and high school at-risk students and helped many of them stay in school and graduate. Karate was also a source of income.

Martial arts helped me promote to the rank of sergeant at the Texas Department of Public Safety-State Trooper Training Academy, where I served for over eight years in the state police training bureau. Karate has been my life and still is today. I am currently working on a program to

TRAINING INFORMATION

- Martial Arts Styles & Ranks: Tae Kwon Do 8th to 10th Dan, Goju 6th to 10th Dan, Hapkido 6th Dan, Police and Military Combat Instructor: Physical Fitness & Defensive Tactics Instructor/Coordinator -Texas Department of Public Safety (State Trooper) agency-wide
- Instructors/Influencers: James Debrow, Jr., Herbert Debrow, Johnny Davis, Masters Choi, Kim & Chang, Dr. Abel Villareal, Professor Charles Dixon, Grand Master Richard Dixon, Grand Master Mike Fillmore, Dr. Dan Roberts
- Birthdate: May 23, 1955
- Birthplace/Growing Up: San Antonio, TX
- Yrs. In the Martial Arts: 61 years
- Yrs. Instructing: 53 years
- School Owner, Manager & Instructor at James Debrow Fighting Tiger School, LLC

PROFESSIONAL ORGANIZATIONS

- Al Francis Karate Organization
- Shinjimasu International Martial Arts Association
- Global Tae Kwon Do Association
- Tae Kwon Do, Yong Moo Kwan Federation
- The World Moo Duk Kwan Alliance-United States Branch of Tae Kwon Do Association

help children with memory, attention span, and concentration skills.

Martial Arts is the best thing that ever happened to me!

BIO

I got started in boxing and martial arts at the age of 4 (1959) years old because my father and two uncles were professional boxers and black belts. My first four black belts ranks were from my father and uncles. Additionally, I studied martial arts while in the United States Army in the Republic of Korea (ROK), Okinawa, and Tokyo, Japan. I was promoted under Dr. Al Francis, 10th Dan black belt, Al Francis Karate Organization 5th Dan to 10 Dan black belt in San Antonio, Texas (1985-2020).

- Shinjimasu International Martial Arts Association, Black Belt Advancement Certificate 9th Dan Black Belt Shaolin Goju ID#Nbq 10137 on July 18, 1993, by Soke Charles Dixon 10th Dan, Chairman of the Council and the Shinjimasu Board of Directors, Temple, Texas.
- Shinjimasu International Martial Arts Association, United Federation of International Grand Masters, Letter of Recognition and Inauguration, Recognized as a 10th Dan Black Belt, Professor of Martial Arts, Lifetime Member on June 22, 2019, by Soke Charles Dixon 10th Dan, Chairman of the Council and the Shinjimasu Board of Directors, Temple, Texas.

PERSONAL ACHIEVEMENTS

- Shinjimasu International Martial Arts Association, Temple, Texas: Golden Life Achievement, Karate Achievement and Black Belt Advancement Certificate (Grand Master Levels)

MAJOR ACHIEVEMENTS

- Physical Fitness and Defensive Tactics Coordinator for the Texas Department of Public Safety-State Trooper Training Academy agency-wide 1994-2003, developed and implemented the physical fitness and wellness program and the defensive tactics program for recruit school cadets and agency incumbents, Use-of-Force Expert/policy developer, Court-certified Use-of-Force, assigned to develop, implement and instruct in the new Texas Conceal Handgun Program at the Texas Department of Public Safety as approved by the Texas Legislatures.
- Philadelphia Historic Martial Arts Society, Martial Arts Hall of Fame inductee Class of 2020; United States Martial Arts, Martial Arts Hall of Fame Inductee Class of 2020; and The Universal Martial Arts Hall of Fame Inductee Class of 2020; Texas Amateur Martial Arts Association-Executive Committee Chair; The World Moo Duk Kwan Do Alliance appointed as Central Director of the National Hapkido Association; and International Police Tactical Training Academy of the International Police Tactical Training Unit

MAJOR ACHIEVEMENTS

- International Police Tactical Training Academy, Appointed International Director of Training of the International Police Tactical Training Unit on June 26, 2020, by President, Grand Master Robert J. Fabrey, 10th Dan Black Belt and President, United States Karate Federation, National Headquarters, St. Portia, Florida. Promoted and registered member of the United States Karate Federation since 1997
- Philadelphia Historic Martial Arts Society, Martial Arts Hall of Fame Inductee Class of 2020.
- United States Martial Arts, Martial Arts Hall of Fame Inductee Class of 2020, and Membership. International Martial Arts Council of America. Hot Springs, Arkansas.
- The Universal Martial Arts Hall of Fame Inductee Class of 2020 and Membership.

Fumio Demura

A master of Shito-ryu Karate and Okinawan Kobudo, Fumio Demura is a true legend and pioneer of American Karate. He has appeared on the front cover of over 30 martial arts magazines. An author of several books, he has also built a successful film career in Hollywood.

Fumio Demura was born in Yokohama Japan on 15 September 1940 to a big family. A shy child, he had four brothers and two sisters.

Aged eight years, Demura began training in Kendo. He had suffered a severe infection of his tonsils that made him very weak. His doctor suggested taking a martial art to help build up his strength.

He started training in Kendo under Asano Sensei, who was his neighbor. He later continued his Kendo training with Master Ryusho Sakagami. Later, Sakagami Sensei also started training Demura in Shito-Ryu Karate-Do. He made a special exception for Demura because, at that time, only adults could train in Karate, but Demura's passion and drive eventually convinced Sakagami Sensei to allow Demura to train.

"Sport Karate is like a game. In traditional Karate you learn human life."

The training was tough at Sakagami's dojo. Even though Demura trained almost every day, he failed his first-ever Karate grading. However, this provided him with a desire to train even harder.

At Sakagami's dojo, Demura studied Kendo under Taisaburo Nakamura. He later studied Kobudo under Shinken Taira, who had

been invited to teach at Sakagami's dojo. Demura credits Taira with much of the Kubodo knowledge he has. In Kendo, Kobudo, and most especially Karate-Do, Sakagami Sensei was an enormous influence in Demura's life.

Following the death of Shito-Ryu founder Kenwa Mabuni in 1952, many of his top students founded their own versions of Shito-Ryu. Sakagami founded the Shito-Ryu Itosu-Kai Organization.

In 1957 the JKA Championships were held for the first time. The tournament was won by Hirokazu Kanazawa. Until this tournament Karate training was purely self-defense purposes. However, the emphasis of training started to change, the focus turning toward keeping Kumite (sparring) in with tournaments in mind. That same year the Demura entered and won the East Japan Championships. A year earlier he had been awarded his 1st Dan by Sakagami.

Ryoichi Sasagawa, of the Japan Karate Federation organized an All-Styles All-Japan Karate championship in 1961, for his Rengokai organization. The tournament was open to all styles of Karate, including Goju-ryu, Shotokan, Shito-ryu and Wado-ryu. Demura entered and won the tournament. From 1961 to 1964 he was considered one of the top eight competitors in the whole of Japan.

Apart from being a student of Sakagami, Demura had the opportunity to train with some of the best Karate and Kobudo Masters in the world this includes:

- Teruo Hayashi – Karate and Kobudo
- Yuchoku Higa – Karate
- Shoshin Nagamine – Karate
- Chosin Chibana – Karate
- Kenei Mabuni – Karate

- Yasuhiro Konishi – Karate and Kendo
- Kenzo Mabuni – Karate
- Shinken Taira – Kobudo
- Motokatsu Inoue – Kobudo

In 1963 the All-Japan Kobudo Taikai (Traditional Weapons Demonstration) was held, with many top Masters in attendance. Sakagami was assisted by Demura at the event. Jojutsu master, Takaji Shimizu and his assistant Donn Draeger were also in attendance. Martial arts historian Draeger became good friends with Demura.

Draeger introduced Demura to Dan Ivan, an early pioneer of Karate in the United States. Demura taught Ivan Kubudo at Draeger's home in Ichigaya, just outside of Tokyo.

In 1964 Ivan invited Demura to come to the United States. However, due to various commitments, Demura could not go. The following year he finally made the move to America, arriving in Los Angeles. Ivan acted as his sponsor. Demura started teaching at Ivan's Shotokan dojo. In respect to Ivan, he learned all the Shotokan kata, to teach them at the dojo. He continued practicing Shotokan until around 1986.

At Ed Parker's annual International Karate Championships held in 1965, Demura gave a demonstration of various Kubodo weapons. The event was featured in Black Belt Magazine. At the event, he also met Chuck Norris for the first time.

1966 saw Demura featured on his first Black Belt Magazine cover. Three years later he was inducted into the Black Belt Hall of Fame as one of the top instructors in the United States. In 1975 he received the Black Belt Hall of Fame Man of the Year Award.

By the 1970s Demura was running his own Shito-Ryu Karate-Do dojo in Los Angeles. He had returned to teaching Shito-Ryu Karate-Do kata and Kubodo. He had become one of the most recognizable faces, giving many demonstrations. He became one of the first masters to use music to display traditional Karate in an innovative approach. However, this approach to traditional Karate faced a lot of criticism, even from his teacher Sakagami.

In 1975, the WUKO World Championships took place at Long Beach, California. During the tournament, Demura gave a Karate demonstration in front of a crowd that included many great Japanese Karate masters. On completion of his demonstration, he received a standing ovation.

As a child, Demura had always wanted to be an actor. However, his father dissuaded him as he felt it would be a difficult path to follow. He never lost the dream to act. He made his acting debut in the 1977 movie, "The Island of Dr Moreau," starring Burt Lancaster and Michael York. He played the part of "Hyena Man."

In the 1984 film, "The Karate Kid" Demura was the stunt double for Pat Morita, who played the enigmatic Mr. Miyagi. Demura and Morita became good friends and over the coming years would work together on various projects. In 1986 they worked on the sequel to "Karate Kid" This was followed in 1989 by "Karate Kid III".

On 6 January 1989 Demura suffered a heart attack during the filming of a fight scene on the TV show O'Hara. He had been pushing himself fairly hard. He was running his successful dojo, while at the same time building a successful career as an actor/stuntman.

In the 1990s Demura continued building his reputation as an actor

and stuntman. In 1993 he appeared in the film Rising Sun. The following year he worked as a stuntman on The Next Karate Kid. In 1995 he worked as a stuntman on Mortal Kombat.

Demura has appeared in a number of documentaries on martial arts. In 1976 he appeared in The Warrior Within as one of fifteen top martial arts practitioners. The masters exhibited their various skills and discussed how they felt about spirituality, philosophy and self-defense.

In 2015 the documentary "The Real Miyagi" was released. Directed by Kevin Derek, the documentary is on the life of Demura. It features interviews with many of the top masters and martial artists who have had the opportunity to know and work with him. The documentary was critically acclaimed, winning a number of awards including the Canada International Film Festival.

Several senior politicians have recognized the impact Demura has had on the development of Karate and Kubodo in America. He has received several official letters of recognition from US president Bill Clinton, George Bush and Barack Obama in 1996, 2005, and 2010 respectively. Demura has also been recognized by the government of Japan, receiving the rare honor of the Japan Foreign Minister's Commendation, Gaimu Daikon, in 2019.

Demura has also received several lifetime achievement awards. In 2000 he received the Golden Life Achievement Award (Excellence in Pioneering) from the World Martial Arts Hall of Fame. In the same year he received achievement awards from the National Association of Professional Martial Artists; United States Karate Alliance; Black Belt Magazine; and special recognition from the US Olympic Committee.

The growth of Karate and Kubodo into a worldwide phenomenon has been a driving force for Demura. As such he has always promoted Karate whenever he has had the chance, through seminars, demonstrations and books. His list of books include:

- Shito-Ryu Karate (1971)
- Advanced Nunchaku (1976)
- Tonfa: Karate Weapon of Self-defense (1982)
- Nunchaku: Karate Weapon of Self-defense (1986)
- Bo: Karate Weapon of Self-defense (1987)
- Sai: Karate weapon of Self-defense (1987)
- More recently, Demura has written books of a more personal nature: "Fumio Demura: My Story," an autobiography, and "10 Rules for a Successful Life," in which he shares his rules and beliefs to help others lead productive, happy lives.

In 1972 Demura helped establish the Invitational Goodwill Karate Championships. An annual traditional Karate event, competitors compete in Kubodo kata and kumite, as well as Karate kata and kumite. There are also seminars and demonstrations given by Demura and other masters at the two-day event.

On 21 February 2015, a special banquet was given to celebrate Demura's 50th anniversary of teaching in the United States. 600 people attended the event. Guests included Tsutomo Ohshima, Tak Kubota, and several Hollywood stars. Rather than being the centre of attention, Demura in characteristic fashion honoured his students. He inducted his most loyal students into the Genbu-kai Hall of Fame. At the end of the night, he expressed his gratitude to the audience.

Now in his 80s, and having adapted to and overcome numerous challenges in enormously inspiring fashion, Demura is still involved in the art he loves. He continues to teach and give demonstrations. He is one of the true pioneers of American Karate. He is one of the most revered and respected masters in the Karate world. He has

helped make Karate a popular and accessible pastime enjoyed by many. Demura continues his ongoing mission to be positive and effective in the lives of people everywhere, and his generosity and presence are experienced by countless people throughout the world.

Source:

http://findingkarate.com/wordpress/spotlight-fumio-demura-the-real-mr-miyagi/

Featuring Over 200 Martial Artists Worldwide

As we read the stories that are captured in this book with over 500 pages, we can all be moved by the inspiration, discipline, heart, passion, focus, and other character qualities that the stories represent. This is not just another anthology or book of stories.

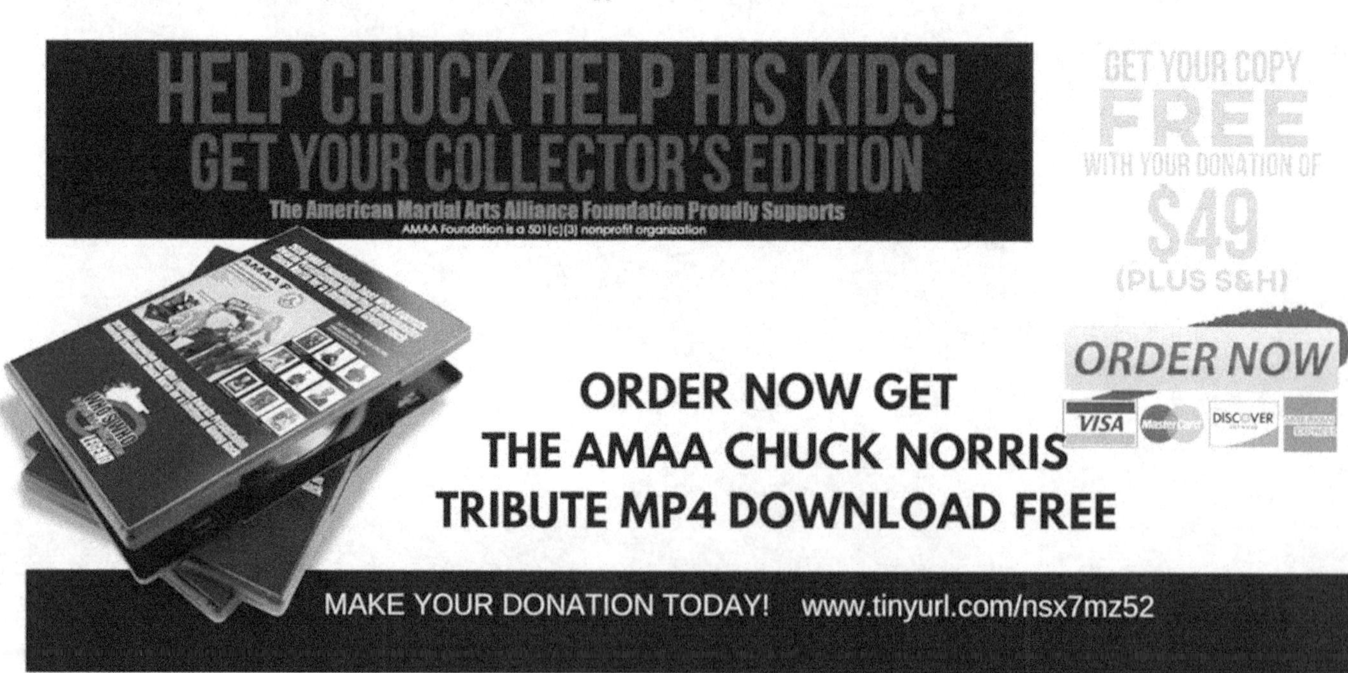

Rayot Difate

"I encourage my older karate comrades to put themselves out there and continue to participate when possible!"

Hachidan Rayot Difate was born in 1941 in Yonkers, New York. He entered the army in 1960 and volunteered for the 101st Airborne Division. Upon being sent to Korea for a period of 3 years, he began the study of Judo. Upon being honorably discharged in 1963, he returned to White Plains, New York to continue his studies in Kyokushin Karate. In 1965, he joined the Yonkers Police Department while continuing his martial arts training. After a one year of intense training program, under Sensei Shigeru Oyama, Rayot became the 1st Black Belt student to be promoted in the US, in 1967, in the style of Kyokushin Karate Do.

In 1976, during an undercover operation with the Yonkers Police Department, Rayot sustained life-threatening injuries, forcing his retirement from the Police Department, due to permanent disabilities followed by years of multiple surgeries. As part of his personal physical and mental rehabilitation, he returned

TRAINING INFORMATION

- Belt Ranks & Martial Arts Styles: World Oyama Karate, 8th Dan
- Instructors/Influencers: Shigeru Oyama (Deceased)
- Birthplace/Growing Up: Yonkers, NY/West Harrison, NY
- Yrs. In the Martial Arts: 61 years
- Yrs. Instructing: 56 years

PROFESSIONAL ORGANIZATIONS

- Yonkers Police Department (Retired 1978)
- Veterans of Foreign War, Post 4037
- American Federation of Martial Arts
- New Breed Life Martial Arts Association
- Eastern USA International Martial Arts Association
- Bushiken Karate

to the dojo with a modified training program. In 1998, he was promoted to the rank of Shihan.

From 1998 to present, Rayot has taught at the White Plains Dojo, under the direction of Shoshu Oyama. Shihan has spent the past 58 years in both the study and instruction of martial arts. On September 10, 2014, after 55 years of training with World Oyama Karate, Shihan Rayot was awarded promotion to 8th Degree Black Belt. He has also been inducted into the American Federation of Martial Arts Hall of Fame, as Diamond Lifetime Achievements in 2013, Ambassador of Goodwill to the Martial Arts in 2014, International Instructor of the Year in 2014, and The New Breed Life Arts Education Association in Harlem, in 2015.

Hachidan has participated and given seminars in the US, Canada, Panama, Haiti, and the Dominican Republic. Upon turning the age of 70, Hachidan decided that his "Bucket List" would consist of competing in 100 tournaments, over the next 5 years. In July of 2017, upon turning 76 years old, he completed this goal. He continues to participate in tournaments in the Tri-State area, displaying his form and techniques in Kata, Weapons, and Self-Defense. He takes great pride in his trophies and medals surrounding his family room. He enjoys membership with the Harrison, New York Veterans of Foreign War.

He continues to be a source of inspiration to other martial artists, wherever he goes, as the oldest competitor, doing

PERSONAL ACHIEVEMENTS

- As of the age of 70 years old: Started and completed 100 tournaments through Age 75 years old, in both national and international competitions. Continues to be one, if not, the oldest Tri-state competitor in New York, New Jersey, and Connecticut. Continues to both train and compete on a regular basis.

MAJOR ACHIEVEMENTS

- Completion of 100 tournaments between the age of 70 and 75, in both national and international Karate tournaments
- Membership in the Harrison, New York, Veterans of Foreign War, Post 4037
- Honorary discharge from the US Army in 1963
- Honorary Retirement from the Yonkers Police Department in 1978
- One, if not the oldest, competitor in the Tri-State Martial Arts Tournaments
- Achievement of 10th Dan in Martial Arts
- 9th Dan presented by Adolfo Ennever, Hanshi/Soke of the American Federation of martial arts on December 3, 2018.
- 9th Dan, by Eastern USA International Arts Association, under Grandmaster John Kanzler, Soke, on November 10, 2018.
- 10th Dan, presented by Grandmaster Lamar Thornton, under New Breed Life Association, October 10, 2015.

what he truly finds both motivating and rewarding. In 2008, at the invitation of Shihan John Turnball, he was accepted into the American Federation of Martial Arts. In 2014, he was conferred the rank of Black Belt 7th Dan. Also, in 2014, he was awarded the rank of 8th Dan by both Shugeru Oyama and the American Federation of Martial Arts. In 2015, he was conferred with the rank of 10th Dan by Grand Master Lamarr Thornton of NBLA. In 2017, he was inducted into the Eastern USA International Martial Arts Association. Presently, Hachidan is a member of Bushiken Karate.

On June 30th 2019, Grandmaster Rayot Difate competed in Hue, Vietnam in a 3-day martial arts tournament sponsored by NGHIA Dung Karate-Do Mo Rong.

This was the first time in 60 years that this Asian tournament was open to Americans. Grandmaster traveled with a party of five, to be only one of two Americans competing.

Grandmaster took third place in Kata and 5th place in weapons. There were 800 competitors over the entire three-day event. He competed in the 50-year and older Masters division, in which he had the honor of being the oldest competitor at the age of 78. Besides representing the USA, were other Asian countries with Australia and Canada. He continues to teach, train, and compete. He encourages his older karate comrades to put themselves out there and continue to participate when possible.

Mike Dillard

Mike Dillard, owner of Century Martial Arts is a martial artist at heart and a businessman by nature. Dillard is an advanced black belt in Taekwondo and Tang Soo Do, a 9th-degree in Kang Duk Won under Roger Greene, and an 8th-degree in Chun Kuk Do under Chuck Norris.

Mr. Dillard graduated from Oklahoma State University in Stillwater, Oklahoma in 1974 with a Bachelor of Science – Major in Accounting. He has done post graduate work at Harvard and Stanford. While attending OSU, Mike studied and taught martial arts, which was the beginning of his 40-plus-year legacy.

While pursuing his passion for martial arts, his business acumen always ran in tandem. In 1976, as a 1st-degree black belt and regional karate champion, he began making quality uniforms out of his garage. Century, the equipment company he founded soon afterward, has since become the world's largest supplier of martial arts products, producing product lines for many martial arts and styles.

> "Mike Dillard is the owner of Century Martial Arts and Black Belt Magazine, the iconic magazine of martial arts practitioners worldwide."

Dillard is affiliated with numerous martial arts organizations, including Chuck Norris' United Fighting Arts Federation (UFAF); Budo-Kai International; United States Martial Arts Association; World Taekwondo Federation; Martial Arts International Federation; and United States Martial Arts Federation. He was a captain of the 1990 UFAF team that went to the USSR, and was

honored as Black Belt magazine's "Man of the Year" in 2011 and inducted into its Hall of Fame. He was also inducted into the Masters Hall of Fame in 2014 and the International Martial Arts Council in 2018.

In 1989, Dillard founded the Dillard Group, a large residential real-estate firm in Cleveland County, OK. He founded Waterford Properties in Oklahoma City in 1995. Waterford is a regional commercial real-estate holding company, which has substantial investments in commercial, office and warehouse real estate.

In 1999, Century purchased Panther Videos. In 2001, Dillard founded the Martial Arts Industry Association (MAIA). Along with its official trade publication MASuccess Magazine, MAIA educates thousands of martial arts school owners and instructors to operate their business more professionally and profitably.

In July 2017 Michael Dillard announced that Century Martial Arts had acquired Black Belt Magazine, the iconic magazine of martial arts practitioners worldwide. At the Gathering of World Changers at the 50th Battle of Atlanta in June 2018, Mike received the Joe Lewis Eternal Warrior award, presented by Bill Wallace, Jeff Smith, and Joe Lewis' daughter Kristina. Also in 2018 Century became the owner of Gameness Jiu Jitsu Gi Brand.

Mr. Dillard's other endeavors have included professional kickboxing; TV and movie stunt work; spearfishing; scuba diving; mountain climbing; golf; hiking; skiing; biking; and professional race-car driving.

He is on the Oklahoma University Board of Advisors, College of Business, and a retired Professor of Business at Oklahoma

University, where he taught Entrepreneurial Business in the MBA Program for ten years. Master Dillard continues to train in the martial arts daily. He teaches seminars and classes at Century's corporate headquarters and also takes part in various martial arts competitions.

Rocky DiRico

"I have been able to stay healthy and have been able to instruct thousands of people in 47 years..."

BIO

I started training martial arts in 1972 with a friend, Steve McGown. Studying the marital arts has impacted my life in many ways. I have been able to stay healthy and have been able to instruct thousands of people in 47 years of teaching. It has been my profession since 1975.

TRAINING INFORMATION

- Martial Arts Styles & Rank: Kenpo Karate, Shito-Ryu Karate, Small Circle JuJitsu, Traditional Kobudo
- Instructors/Influencers: Professor Nick Cerio, Sensei Brian Ricci, Professor Dave Castoldi
- Birthdate: August 6, 1952
- Birthplace/Growing Up: Italy / Watertown, MA
- Yrs. In the Martial Arts: 59 years
- Yrs. Instructing: 47 years
- School owner

PROFESSIONAL ORGANIZATIONS

- Team Paul Mitchell
- World Martial Arts Association
- (Board Member)
- National Museum of Sport Karate
- (History General)
- K.R.A.N.E. official

PERSONAL ACHIEVEMENTS

- Won over 50 National & World titles
- NASKA, NBL, PkL & KRANE Champion
- Induction in 14 Halls of Fame
- Promoted over 500 Black Belts

MAJOR ACHIEVEMENTS

- Winner of Official Karate Magazine's
- SHUTO AWARD
- Part in movie: The Last Operative
- First "Senior" to win Grand Championship at a NASKA, NBL and PKL event
- Competitor of the year: 1990
- Karate teacher of the year: 2007

Robert Dunn

PERSONAL & MAJOR ACHIEVEMENTS

- Grandmaster Robert Dunn started his Martial Arts training in 1962, where Grandmaster Parker Shelton once owned a School in North Carolina.
- In 1969, Grandmaster Robert Dunn was introduced to Grandmaster Kong Young Il a Pioneer in the Art of Taekwon-Do and started his training in Taekwon-Do under the direction of Grandmaster Kong Young Il.
- In 1970, Grandmaster Robert Dunn opened his first Taekwon-Do school
- In 1977, Grandmaster Robert Dunn met Grandmaster Ahn Eung Choon and started training under him.
- In 1987, Grandmaster Ahn Eung Choon certified Grandmaster Robert Dunn as an International Judge.
- In 1988, Grandmaster Robert Dunn was inducted into the International Karate Hall of Fame by Dan Soward, the president of the International Karate Hall of Fame in Las Vegas, Nevada.
- 1989, Grandmaster Robert Dunn was contracted to teach the Art of Taekwon-Do to Peruvian troops in Lima, Peru.

TRAINING INFORMATION

- Belt Ranks & Martial Arts Styles: Tae Kwon Do (9th Degree Black Belt)
- Instructors/Influencers: Grand Master Kong Young II
- Birthplace/Growing Up: Chester, PA
- Yrs. In the Martial Arts: 58 years
- Yrs. Instructing: 55 years

PROFESSIONAL ORGANIZATIONS

- International Juntong Tae Kwon-Do Federation

PERSONAL & MAJOR ACHIEVEMENTS

- Grandmaster Robert Dunn competed in Regional and National level tournaments during the late 1960's and early 1970's.
- Grandmaster Robert Dunn has competed with and trained and received seminars from many of the pioneers in the Martial Arts.

PERSONAL ACHIEVEMENTS

- 2009, on February 21st Grandmaster Robert Dunn was promoted to Grandmaster 9th. Dan Black Belt by Grandmaster Eung Choon Ahn in Macon, Georgia
- 2013, Grandmaster Robert Dunn was inducted into the Black Belt Karate Hall of Fame by Jeff Helaney the president of the Black Belt Hall of Fame in Omaha, Nebraska
- 2013, Grandmaster Robert Dunn establishes a European International Headquarters in the United Kingdom.
- 2013, Grandmaster Robert Dunn establishes a Caribbean International Headquarters in Cabo Rojo, Puerto Rico.
- 2014, Grandmaster Robert Dunn establishes a Israeli International Headquarters in Hoshmonaim, Israel.
- 2014, Grandmaster Robert Dunn has now established International JTF schools in a number of countries around the world
- 2014, Grandmaster Robert Dunn is Recognized by the Black Belt Hall of Fame and Awarded the Pioneer & Legends Award from Grandmaster Jeff Helaney.
- 2017, Grandmaster Robert Dunn is Inducted into the Official Taekwon-Do Hall of Fame and Recognized as a Pioneer of Taekwon-Do in the New York City Ceremony.
- 2018, Grandmaster Robert Dunn travels to Southeast Asia to train Black Belts in the Philippines and train with Grandmaster Kong Young Il in Vietnam.
- 2018, Grandmaster Robert Dunn is appointed as Secretary General of the Young Brothers Taekwon-Do International (YBTI) by Grandmaster Kong Young IL - International Headquarters in Kuala Lumpur, Malaysia.
- 2018, Grandmaster Robert Dunn was inducted into the 2018 "Who's Who" in Martial Arts in a ceremony in Washington, DC.
- 2019, Grandmaster Robert Dunn was selected to be inducted into the "The Book of Grandmasters", sanctioned by the United States National Grandmasters Federation.

PERSONAL ACHIEVEMENTS

- 2019, Grandmaster Robert Dunn was Honored in the 2019 "Who's Who" in Martial Arts in a ceremony in Las Vegas, Nevada.
- 2019, Grandmaster Robert Dunn attends the Taekwon-Do Hall of Fame Ceremonies in Bangkok, Thailand with 4 of his students that have become Grandmasters for their Induction.

Thomas Fleming

"Over my life time Karate has made me who I am, it has become a way of life for me."

Over my life time Karate has made me who I am, it has become a way of life for me. From teaching my classes each day, traveling to competitions seminars we run for the CKA. It has taught me to respect all arts and people and has given me the confidence to overcome great obstacles and never give up always keep going.

BIO

My grandmother started me in Judo at the age of nine years old in 1961 at the YMCA in Ottawa to help me develop my confidence. At the age of 11, I watched Sensei George Sylvian perform a self-defense demonstration at the Ottawa Exposition and was amazed at his control and ask my grandmother if I could join his Karate club which I did and stay with him till I got my Shodan from the Canadian karate Association. When Sensei George Sylvain quit karate to continue his career in Jiujitsu and with a letter of recommendation from him to Sensei Fern Cleroux I joined the Cleroux Karate Club and remained

TRAINING INFORMATION

- Martial Arts Styles & Rank: Shotokan, Chito-ryu, Chito -Shin Kai and Cleroux Karate Do-Shodan to Kudan, Kyoshi and Hanshi ranks
- Instructors/Influencers: Professor George Sylvain, Hanshi Fern Cleroux, OSensei Tsuruoka
- Birthdate: June 12, 1952
- Birthplace/Growing Up: Ottawa, Canada
- Yrs. In the Martial Arts: 59 years
- Yrs. Instructing: 53 years
- School owner at Fleming Karate Clubs

PROFESSIONAL ORGANIZATIONS

- Canadian Karate Association since 1971- VP Since 1982 to 2013, President from 2013 to 2020, Past President 2021

his student for over 50 years until his death. I still honor him and wear his crest on all my Gis Cleroux Karate Club and call our style Cleroux Karate Do as he was the greatest influence in my life and career as an instructor and dear friend.

PERSONAL ACHIEVEMENTS

- Competed in Regional Provincial National and International competitions in Kumite Kata Breaking, and Weapons and demonstration teams. We were called the Cleroux Power Team

MAJOR ACHIEVEMENTS

- Being involved in the Canadian Karate Association over the years and becoming President and working with and meeting some of the greatest people I now have the pleasure to call my friends. But my greatest achievement has been as an Instructor these past 53 years teaching men, women and children, watching them grow and their excitement achieving their goals.

Ted Gambordella

"During the last 10 years I began to recognize the World's Greatest Martial Artists and started doing tribute videos, over 500 so far..."

BIO

My brothers used to beat me up so I started to learn to defend myself ... and they never beat me up again.

I started my Martial Arts journey in Alexandria, Louisiana in 1964 training under a man named Bill Hawthorne, in Shorindo Karate. This was during the Vietnam War, and the only people who knew martial arts were military people.

I earned my first Black Belt in 1968 in Okinawan Karate and during that time I met Soke Rod Sacharnoski, now famous for Combat Ki, at a class at LSU-A. I went there to beat him up since I had heard he was telling people how he could take full power punches and kicks and rather berating traditional karate. I soon changed my mind after I kicked him in the groin, smashed his ribs, and gave a vicious Shuto to the throat and the only thing that was hurt was my hand and foot. I became Soke's third Black Belt in America, and went to live with him in North

TRAINING INFORMATION

- Belt Ranks & Martial Arts Styles: 10th Degree Juko Ryu Jiu Jitsu...Soke (Head of Family), 10th Degree Aiki Jitsu, 10th Degree Okinawan Karate, 8th Degree Tae Kwon Do, 8th Degree Weapons
- Instructors/Influencers: Bill Hawthorne, Soke Rod Sacharnoski, Soke Albert Church, Allen Steen, Royce Young, Keith Yates, James Toney, Vince Tamura, Carlos Machado
- Birthdate: February 22, 1948
- Birthplace/Growing Up: New Haven, CT / Alexandria, LA
- Yrs. In the Martial Arts: 58 years
- Yrs. Instructing: 58 years
- Instructor, Member of PKA Worldwide

PROFESSIONAL ORGANIZATIONS

- PKA Worldwide

Carolina where I meet one of his teachers, Soke Albert Church, a great man and teacher. Soke Church had a 100-year old scroll giving him his Sokeship.

I became a weapons black belt and 2nd degree Jiu Jitsu Black Belt under Soke Church. There were very few martial arts schools in Louisiana then, and only one was Karl Marx school in Alexandria. There were no jiu jitsu schools in existence in Louisiana, or in the South.

I started the first Jiu Jitsu Club at LSU and was the first teacher to promote students to Black Belt in Jiu Jitsu, and weapons in the South. I started the first karate tournament at the college, the Southern Karate Championship.

At LSU I meet and trained with Dr. He Young Kimm, the great Hapikdo teacher and I was the first man to get a Doctorate from LSU in Martial Arts History.

I wrote my first book on the Martial Arts in 1975, The End of Injury, and traveled around the southern United States to work with colleges and professional teams to help prevent injuries in sports. I was endorsed by LSU, OU, OSU, Rice, Perdue, Alabama, Oral Roberts U, Louisiana College, The Houston Rockets, The New Orleans Jazz, and dozens of high schools.

During that time I developed my famous KI demonstrations. I would let the largest men hit me in the throat, groin, ribs, and solar plexus with no injury to me. I also became famous for knocking apples out of people mouths with nunchakus and bending a 12 inch razor

PERSONAL ACHIEVEMENTS

- 1st Black Belt 1968
- World Martial Arts Hall of Fame 1998
- Grandmaster Instructor of the Year 2000
- International Weapons Master Instructor of Year 2001
- Martial Arts Weapons Hall of Fame 2001
- World Head of Family Sokeship Council 1999
- Martial Art Legends Hall of Fame 2001
- Martial Arts Masters Hall of Fame 2002
- World Black Belt Hall of Fame 2003
- Personal Trainers Hall of Fame 2007
- Karate Masters Hall of Fame 2011
- Masters Hall of Fame 2014
- Joe Lewis Award from Joe Corley, 2017
- Patented Inventor

MAJOR ACHIEVEMENTS

- Author of 75 books and 42 DVDs
  1st Jiu Jitsu Black Belt in Texas
- 1st weapons Black Belt in Texas, and Louisiana
- 1st Okinawan Karate Black Belt in Louisiana
- 1st to promote others to black belt in weapons and jiu jitsu in Texas and Louisiana
- 1st jiu jitsu team in Louisiana and Texas
- 1st Jiu Jitsu Black Belt at Louisiana State University
- Started first Jiu Jitsu club at LSU
- Produced 1st Karate Collegiate Championship tournament 1971
- 1st author of book on Hard KI (chi)
- 1st person to bend knife on neck in demonstration
- Wrote the 1st Complete Martial Arts Weapons manual in 1976, best-selling martial arts manual in history, still in print after 35 years
- Wrote 1st book on using martial arts techniques in sports to prevent injuries, improve performance and develop a winning attitude. Which was used and endorsed by University of Texas, OU, LSU, Oral Roberts, Louisiana College, Purdue, Rice University, Houston Rockets, New Orleans Jazz, dozens of high schools

sharp butcher knife on my neck.

I was promoted to 5th degree by Soke Sacharnoski, and moved to Texas in the 1980s. I had a martial arts school in Wichita Falls, Texas and came to Dallas to do a demo in Allen Steen's US Karate Open, and Pat Burleson's Texas Karate Championship. I was very successful with my demos and was the only man in the 25 years of Allen Steen's tournament to demonstrate for five years in a row. I also did demos at George Minshew's Karate Olympics and all the other major tournaments in Texas and Louisiana.

I wrote my two most successful Martial Arts books during the 1980s, The 100 Deadliest Karate Moves, and The Complete Book of Karate Weapons. They sold 100,000+ copies and I began writing for Paladin Press who published eight more of my titles.

I produced the first digital martial arts books in 1986 at the start of the Internet. And then I produced the first digital Martial Arts CD, The Ultimate Martial Arts CD with 32 books, and five hours of video. And I had one of the first martial arts web pages, WWWIN.com. There was no streaming and only slow modems back then, so you could not do high quality online material.

I have been considered a fitness pioneer and operated some of the largest health clubs in Louisiana, and Texas for several years. I have been working out, eating right, and continually training for 45 years and look better today than I did 20 years ago.

MAJOR ACHIEVEMENTS

- 1st Martial Arts black belt with a weekly TV show in America, 2 years on channel 11 DFW
- Voted "The Most Perfect Body in America 1980"
- Appeared on National TV 8 times with martial arts programs including Real People, Entertainment Tonight, Playboy Channel, Fox TV,
- Inside Edition, and dozens of local TV stations across Texas and Louisiana
- 1st Martial Arts Master to work with US Olympic committee training US Olympic athletes using martial arts techniques
- 1st Jiu Jitsu demonstration at the Karate Olympics, US Karate Championship, Mardi Gras Nationals, Texas Karate Championships, Big D, (5 years in a row; no one had ever done more than three before), and dozens of other tournaments
- Featured in Black Belt Magazine, Inside Kung Fu, and Martial Arts Business cover story
- 1st American author of karate weapons manual
  1st author to produce martial art book digitally in 1990
  1st martial arts master author with Iphone application
  1st martial arts master with Video's and DVD's
  1st web site for martial arts books and videos 1990
- 1st martial arts author to sell digital books on Ebay
- Inventor with Patented products, Logo Glove and Vpower glove
- Started the Martial Arts Masters Hall of Fame 1992
- Started the first Martial Arts MLM "winners club" in 1982
- Invented the "Gambretta" the ultimate legal carry self-defense weapon
- TV Pilot Live2B100 in 2008
- Author of The World's Greatest Martial Artists...19 Volumes...honoring over 1,900 Great Martial Artists and counting

50 YEARS OF MARTIAL ARTS EXCELLENCE

I was inducted into the Personal Trainer Hall of Fame, and have appeared on National TV several times with my fitness books, martial arts, and motivational books.

I have written 75+ plus books on the Martial Arts and produced over 40 DVDs as well as 2,000 videos on You Tube.

During the last 10 years I began to recognize the world's greatest martial artists and started doing tribute videos, over 500 so far, and writing my book series The World's Greatest Martial Artists. I have done 19 volumes of the book now.

I wrote the End of Injury, the first book on using martial arts techniques in sports to prevent injuries, improve performance and develop a winning attitude. It was used and endorsed by University of Texas, OU, LSU, Oral Roberts, Louisiana College, Purdue, Rice University, Houston Rockets, New Orleans Jazz, and dozens of high schools.

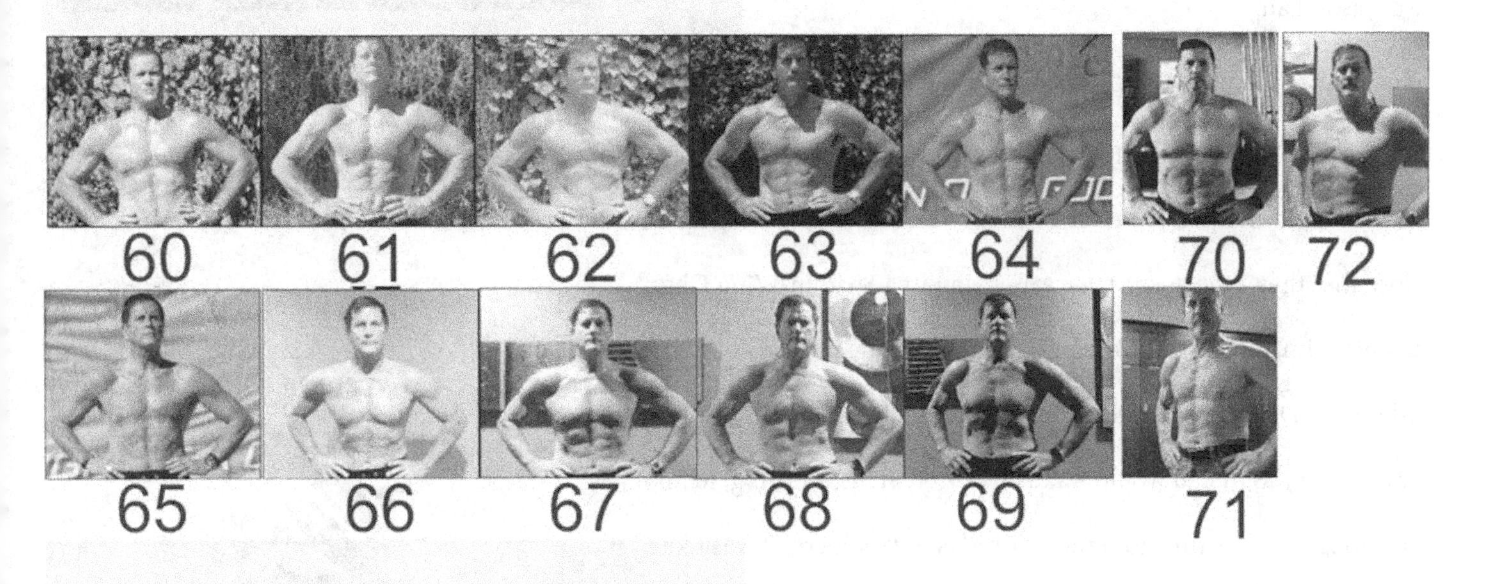

Alan Goldberg

One must wonder what Master Goldberg, publisher and promoter of the event is thinking looking out in this vast sea of martial artists. How did it all start? Over fifty years ago Alan Goldberg set forth on a path in Martial Arts that some of us could only dream of. Master Goldberg's early training was in the art of Shotokan Karate and he studied with Masters Manard Miner and George Cofield. He would later learn the traditional and non-traditional arts of Five Animal Kung Fu.

As the 1970s entered, Master Goldberg met a young Master who took him on the path to where he is at today. That young Master was Jason Lau.

As the 1970s entered, Master Goldberg met a young Master who took him on the path to where he is at today. That young Master was Jason Lau.

Sifu Lau is the disciple of famed Shaw Brothers stable, Master Jiu Wan. Sifu Lau and Master Goldberg would form a student and Master bond that has lasted over thirty years. Their friendship so close that they even spent five years living in a Shaolin Wing Chun temple with three other disciples, and Master Lau now holds the title of #1 Disciple of the Family. Master Goldberg jokes of those days saying, "Sifu Lau would wake up at 2:00 in the morning, telling his disciples it was time to train." For Master Goldberg, it was like a dream. But sometimes woke up the next morning wondering was it

or wasn't it. "I would have lived there longer with Sifu Lau, but I was due to get married soon and my wife did not agree with my continued plan of living in a temple." (And he wonders why not…)

When Sifu Lau left New York City in the early 80s, he suggested Master Goldberg train with the late Sifu Moy Yat of the Yip Man family. This would give Master Goldberg the opportunity to study Wing Chun under different Sifus and allow him the chance to have a well-rounded education in the art. Known for his longevity in the art, Master Goldberg is a pioneer of Wing Chun in the United States.

Master Goldberg now teaches Wing Chun Kung Fu in the heart of Brooklyn to a small but dedicated group of students. The temple has been active for over 25 years and there have been opportunities to expand it as a business. "I have had opportunities to expand, but I am really not interested in having a large school because it loses some of the tradition and close family ties that I have built with my students," Master Goldberg tells us. The tradition continues as three of his oldest disciples teach in different areas of the United Stated. Master Goldberg's other notable students include actor Joe Piscopo of Saturday Night Live, Heavy-weight World Champion Dimitrius "Oak tree" Edwards who is notoriously known as the man who broke Mike Tyson's ribs in a sparring match, and world renown orthopedic surgeon Dr. Richard Pearl. Others associated with his kung fu family include Phil Morris from Seinfeld, and Joe Venerrie from the oldies group the Tokens.

Master Goldberg is the holder of Black Belt Magazine's "Kung Fu Instructor of the Year – 2004" award, and has been inducted into 70 other Halls of Fame. He holds a position on boards in major martial arts federations. He is a founding member of Martial Arts Grand Master International Council (MAGIC), a founding member of World Black Belt along with Chuck Norris and Bob Wall and he is a board member of the International Sports Hall of Fame with Dr. Bob Goldman and Arnold Schwarzenegger

Publisher of Action Martial Arts Magazine, the largest free magazine in the United States today, he created one of the nation's hottest martial arts fads, Action Martial Arts Magazine Collector Cards. Master Goldberg created Law Enforcement Survival System (LESS), the only self-defense course taught to the NYC Emergency Service Unit of the New York Police Department. He starred in Great Karate Inspirations was the only person performing Kung Fu. He has an instructional video on Wing Chun produced by Yamazato Productions, and appears in Rising Suns' production Martial Arts Masters. He has also taken a position as Vice-President of Shaolin Brand Products, is a board member of the Martial Arts History Museum, the Martial Arts of China Historical Society, and Black Belt Magazine's Festival of Martial Arts, and is Co-President of Sidekick Publications.

He was also one of the promoters and Vice-President of 21st Century Warriors, which showcased some of the legendary martial artists of our time. This event saw the return of Don "The Dragon" Wilson, Royler Gracie, Orlando "The Warrior" Rivera, Dan "The Beast" Severn and others battling it out on Pay-Per View.

His proudest moment is yet to come at the Atlantic City Tropicana Casino and Resort, when he will again produce his MEGA Martial Arts weekend showcasing the Action Martial Arts Magazine Hall of Fame Banquet, and the world's largest martial arts trade show and expo.

John Hawk

"Karate has taught me to stick to what I start until a full conclusion and maintain that level of professionalism ..."

BIO

Originally looking for a judo school at the time I had no idea about Karate or that the art even existed. I was on active duty in the Army in 1965 and thought that art would better my abilities physically. My judo instructor, John Graham, received orders to Vietnam and was killed in action there in 1967. During my last lesson with Sensei Graham, a young fellow by the name of George Chalian, was doing a funny dance in the corner of the wrestling room in the Ft Monmouth, NJ gym. He approached me and told me he could teach me Karate, I said OK and a lifelong passion was born.

Karate has taught me to stick to what I start until a full conclusion and maintain that level of professionalism as a lifelong endeavor by following the BKG motto "begin and persevere."

I also follow our Wado Shinzen-Kai motto "karate" keep a respectful attitude toward. Everyone"

TRAINING INFORMATION

- Martial Arts Styles & Rank: Kodokan Judo to 1st Kyu Brown Belt, 1967, Beikoku Karate do (BKG), Shodan 1969, Nidan 1971, Sandan 1974, Beikoku Karate Do Renmei, Yodan 1975, Godan 1978, Uska Reg#8-64-72, Rokudan 1984, Sichidan 1992, Hachidan 2006 Iama, Kudan 2011 Iama, Judan 2017 Co- Signed By 10 GM's (Including Shihan's Kathy Henry, Gary Alexander, Roy Kurban), Goshindo Kempo Karate, Godan Renshi August 1984 (GM Pete Siringano Sr.)
- Instructors/Influencers: Shihan Isaac Henry Jr., Hanshi George Chalian, GM Robert Trias, GM Roberta Trias, GM Gary Alexander
- Birthdate: January 21, 1942
- Birthplace/Growing Up: Toledo, OH / Hillsdale, MI
- Yrs. In the Martial Arts: 56 years
- Yrs. Instructing: 51 years
- Instructor, Founder of Wado Shinzen-Kai Kokusai

PROFESSIONAL ORGANIZATIONS

- The Honorable Order Of St. Michael (Aviation) 2010
- Aviation: Inducted into the Who's Who of Professionals in 2000

PERSONAL & MAJOR ACHIEVEMENTS

- International Association Of Martial Artists Sr. Member Board Of Governors
- I received the Lifetime Achievement award from the International Association of Martial Artists in 2007 the Lifetime Achievement award from the Beikoku Karate Do Goyukai (BKG) in 2009, inducted into the World Karate Union Hall of Fame 2014, Ambassador of the Martial Arts at Action Martial Arts Magazine 2014, also he received the Meritorious Service Medallion from the International Armed Forces Judo and Jujitsu Academy in 2015 Medallion #72 out of 100 issued in five countries. Shodai Hawk co-sponsored the 1st USKA European tour in 1971 which included GM Robert Trias, Bill "Superfoot" Wallace, Glenn Keeney, Wally Sloki, Robert Bowles and James Fraser to mention a few. He is listed in the SHURI-RYU KARATE BOOK by GM R.A. Trias ``The Pinnacle of Karate" Okinawan Methods of Shuri-ryu circa 1965-69, published 1980 revised 1988 and in Grand Master Gary Alexander's book "Trailblazer 1" in 2014, Action Martial Arts Magazine HALL OF HONORS 2020 pg 143, and WORLD'S GREATEST Vol 21

Stephen K. Hayes

Stephen K. Hayes began his formal training in the Asian martial arts as a teenager in the 1960s. By the autumn of 1985, he had earned a place in the prestigious Black Belt Hall of Fame, honoring him for his years of pioneering work introducing the Japanese ninja martial art of "accomplishment through invisible action" to the American public.

He was awarded the extremely rare Ju-dan Tenth Degree Black Belt in ninja martial arts by grandmaster Masaaki Hatsumi of Chiba, Japan, and Shugendo highest title Dai Sendatsu Grand Path Leader by Shokai Koshikidake of Yamagata, Japan.

He is the founder of the martial art of To-Shin Do, a mind and body self-protection system based on the ancient ninja martial arts principles updated for application to modern 21st Century threats and pressures.

Stephen K. Hayes was born in Wilmington, Delaware, in 1949, and grew up in Dayton, Ohio. He has traveled throughout North America, Europe, the Arctic, Japan, China, Tibet, Nepal, and India. A husband and grandfather, he is a writer, teacher, and ardent student of life.

A 1971 graduate of Miami University in Oxford, Ohio, he majored in speech and theater. Most notable to American audiences was his role beside Richard Chamberlain in the NBC mini-series Shogun.

Stephen K. Hayes is the author of 21 books. Several of his volumes

"We must work to cultivate a state of fearlessness in recognition of the reality that there will be times when things do not go the way we wish them to. We can learn to live positively and generate the results we need in life by creating a momentum of accomplishment."

have been published in a variety of different foreign languages as well. His biography appears in the international edition of Who's Who.

He has served as personal protection agent and security advisor for foreign governments, royal families, and such personalities as the Dalai Lama of Tibet, 1989 winner of the Nobel Peace Prize.

Stephen K. Hayes' and his wife Rumiko oversee a network of training centers and a publishing company dedicated to the sciences of self-development.

Much of the year, he travels the world as a teacher, seminar leader, and lecturer.

His informative and inspiring presentations translate his extensive background in the martial and meditation arts into practical lessons for handling the pressures, choices, uncertainties, and stresses of life in the modern western world.

Stephen K. Hayes' interpretation of Japan's ancient warrior path of enlightenment creates a basis for understanding the power of directed intention as a tool for accomplishment. He emphasizes to audiences around the world:

"We must work to cultivate a state of fearlessness in recognition of the reality that there will be times when things do not go the way we wish them to. We can learn to live positively and generate the results we need in life by creating a momentum of accomplishment. Our ninja martial art training program shows us how to begin. It is then up to our own resourcefulness and commitment as to how far we take ourselves." - Stephen K. Hayes

Art Heller

> "TM Martial Arts Academy focuses on teaching character development, self-defense skills, and developing strong leadership skills..."

BIO

My older brother studied under Jhoon Rhee and Allen Steen at the University of Texas and influenced my younger brother and I to sign up with Allen Steen when he opened up teaching in Highland Park/Dallas Texas in 1962.

My brother John and I were blessed to have studied Tae Kwon Do under GM Allen Steen and became his early 1960's Black Belts. I taught for years under GM Steen at Texas Instruments and Texas Karate Institute. Allen Steen utilized building block principles in teaching karate. My life took a steady building block progression of successful events after beginning studies of karate under Grandmaster Allen Steen. I utilized these building block principles that Grandmaster Steen taught to work my way through college and made high grades graduating with honors. Teaching karate at TKI financed my college education. I went on to do post graduate studies and

TRAINING INFORMATION

- Martial Arts Title: Grand Master
- Currently Resides: Acworth, GA
- Started Studying Martial Arts in 1962
- Instructing Martial Arts for 20 years and currently holds the rank of 10th Degree Black Belt studying martial arts styles: Tae Kwon Do American Karate
- Instructor: Grand Master Allen Steen

PERSONAL ACHIEVEMENTS

- Joe Corley said of Master Heller: "Art Heller was one of the most ferocious fighters of the 1960-70's era. He certainly made me tougher and super respectful of his Texas "upbringing". He was widely respected and widely known for his jump round kick- spinning back kick, both for accuracy and effect. His fearless performances often brought spectators to a standing ovation. His power was dynamic, effective and respected. Some competitors bowed out rather than to compete with Mr. Heller, once called "Mean Man of the South."

became very productive with the positive attitude and goal setting principles that I had acquired. This training poured over into the business world when I had my own companies and while working with Lockheed-Martin GA as Senior Procurement Manager.

Subsequent rewards have been significant.

At age two I was attacked by polio and unable to walk until five years of age.

My mother encouraged me to engage in numerous sports and activities. This as well as the heavy physical labor required in the landscape business and karate were the answers to gaining strength and health. While training in karate I was recognized for my efforts, power and unique flying techniques.

After moving to Georgia, I formed the Southern Black Belt Alliance. Then, as fortune would have it, GM Joe Corley and I formed the SEKA - South East Karate Association. We were joined by Jack Motley, Larry Reinhardt, Sam Chapman, Bill McDonald and many others. This organization sponsored ten tournaments per year in the South East and developed uniform competition rules as well as proficient judges for competition. Karate really began to grow and flourish with formation of the SEKA. I sponsored a number of successful tournaments at Georgia Tech, and became well known for maintaining strong competition, rigid rules and fair judging. SEKA success was magnified by Joe Corley's efforts and his Battle of Atlanta and its continued success.

BIO (continued)

My philosophy towards the martial arts is "Set your goals, work out hard, and achieve goals to better yourself. Then apply this to life. Keep your mind sharp. Moderate, but be practical. Take in what is laid out before you and think about your reactions and objectives in life. LIVE BY EXAMPLE."

My heritage, as developed under Allen Steen has remained intact and has never failed me. Setting examples for people gains respect and makes people think about what they want to do and accomplish. This is probably the most single important thing that people need to learn early in life. Living by example is important. I developed CONFIDENCE, COURAGE, DISCIPLINE, HONOR and INTEGRITY. These assets are extremely important to integrate into your development. To be successful you have to have all of these principles PLUS. Being able to stand on your own requires all of the above. I gave numerous demonstrations over the years. I taught police class techniques. A number of high school and college football players studied under me to improve performance. But, most rewarding was watching poor grade average students improve their life by taking karate and applying the principals learned in class.

Major tournaments that I've participated in include SWK- BBA Championships x2, Oklahoma Open Karate Tournament, University of Texas Karate

Tournament, N. Texas Open Karate Tournament, Atlanta Open Karate Tournament, Battle of Atlanta x2, Pensacola Open Karate Tournament x2, Jhoon Rhee Nationals x2, Tarheel Open Karate Tournament x3, Chattanooga Open, Ole Miss. Karate Tournament and more. Major Achievements: Making BLACK BELT under Grandmaster Allen Steen was major, teaching my way through college was major, becoming Director of the Southern Black Belt Alliance and then the Co-Director of the South East Karate Association with Grand Master Joe Corley was major, recognition by students and peers were major accomplishments, as well as induction to Living Legends Hall of Fame, induction to USA Martial Arts Hall of Fame, and receiving the Joe Lew- is Eternal Fighter Award.

I further received recognition as a 1960-70's fighter in the era of BLOOD and GUTS, article in Karate Illustrated 1970, Director Southern Black Belt Alliance, Co-Director of the SEKA, and various appreciation awards from peers and students. But the greatest achievement and reward was receiving 10th Black Belt from GM Allen Steen and GM Pat Burleson on June 16, 2018!

Moving forward: It is my hope that many of the principles we used to build the SEKA and subsequently martial arts competitors and competition here in the South, will continue to be utilized by today's instructors, organizers and officials. They were powerful principles that will continue to serve martial arts well at all levels.

Johnny Hunter

"Martial Arts rescued me from the streets and provided me with the strength and courage to face all of my fears."

Karate has helped shape me into the man I am today. As a father, teacher, and entrepreneur, it rescued me from the streets and provided me with the strength and courage to face all of my fears. This includes the bullies. Now I am going back to help others achieve the same goals.

BIO

I began practicing martial arts in the schoolyard. My first teacher was my Uncle Leroy Hunter, and when he was no longer able to teach me, he enrolled me at GM Percy Mungu, where I stayed until I was an adult and continued to learn under Shotokan Master Osamu Ozawa, who personally trained and taught me in Shotokan. I am currently the President of the US TKIC, the organization which he founded.

TRAINING INFORMATION

- Martial Arts Styles & Rank: Shotokan Karate-do 8th Dan UMHoF Soke Council, Shotokan US TKIC 6th Dan, US TKIC., Shotokan/Kempo 10th Dan. BDFS Soke Council.
- Instructors/Influencers: Sensei Leroy Hunter, GM Percy Mungu, Shihan Osamu Ozawa
- Birthdate: June 23, 1962
- Birthplace/Growing Up: Houston, TX
- Yrs. In the Martial Arts: 52 years
- Yrs. Instructing: 35 years
- School owner, Manager & Instructor at Hunter Shotokan Kempo Karate School

PROFESSIONAL ORGANIZATIONS

- President of the US TKIC (Traditional Karate International Confederation)

PERSONAL ACHIEVEMENTS

- 1988 AOK Champion 4th in State of Texas
- 1988 NASKA 9th in the National Rating.
- 1997 and 2012 Inducted in the Universal Martial Hall of Fame and gave Karate Seminar.
- 2004 Received and Appreciation Award from City of Houston.
- 2015 Received Award and Gave Seminar at the Genesis International Hall of Fame in Rhode Island.
- 2015 Attended Karate Demo at the Kung Fu and Karate Expo in Atlanta City, NJ
- 2017 Received an Award from Action Martial Arts Hall of Honor.
- 2017 Received Award from the Black Belts Elite Hall of Fame and Inducted onto the Grandmaster Cup in Fresno, CA

MAJOR ACHIEVEMENTS

- Member of the Black Dragon Fighting Society
- Member of the Black Locust and Member of the Grandmaster Council.
- Award from Kungfu and Karate Expo
- Award from the Genesis International Hall of Fame
- Open The 1st free standing Dojo in the Houston Fifth Ward
- Featured on Channel 13 News for making a difference.
- Taught Karate for the 5th Ward Enrichment Program for at risk Boys
- Ambassador for the Sport Karate Museum
- 2017/2018/ Inducted into Who's Who Legends Book and received the Legends Award and Ring
- 2018 Inducted into the Action Martial Arts Magazine Hall of Honors
- 2020/2021 Elected as the President of the US TKIC (Traditional Karate International Confederation)

Larry Isaac

Martial Arts has been, and continues to be, a part of his life for well over 40 years. This retired M/Sgt. has been a black belt longer than most involved in the martial arts has been alive. Although he has been around a "few years" it has only been the last 10 years or so that he came to realize that the promotion in 1968 was "just a piece of paper."

"The Everything has a past, a present and a future. Regardless of the opinions, we must always remember, just as with the clock, the car, and the airplane, someone or somebody started it and others have taken the ball and worked to make it better."

At a young age of 60, Shihan Isaac truly understands the "old" Marine Corp saying, "If you can't run with the dogs, stay on the porch." Well, according to him, he has been "under the porch," and although he may know a little something at age 60, he says he has only recently gotten the permission to "sit on the porch!" Such is the way of "Undondi" the old way. For those who are familiar with the term "Uchinadi" (Uchinandi) or "Koryu" (Tanme), they have been to the "Island of Shangri-La" (Okinawa).

A great Okinawan master was puzzled by the mindset of the young Marines who thought "50" years or even "60" years was old. This young "73" year old Master is quoted as saying (a saying found in many books of the orient), "At 70, you are but a child, at 80, you are merely a youth and at 90, if the ancestors invite you into heaven, ask them to wait until you are 100—and then you might consider it."

This is the very reason why in the traditional Okinawan dialect (Hogan) the word "retirement" does not exist. The style of Karate Shihan Isaac practices, teaches, and continues to learn daily is called

"Okinawa Kenpo Karate-Kobudo." Kenpo (Kempo) with its roots in Chinese Quan-fa is translated as "Fist Way" or "Fist Law." "Kobudo" is translated to mean "Ko" weapons or old and "Budo" as "Martial Arts Way," thus "Kobudo" is translated to mean "The Weapons of the Martial Arts Way."

In 1968 and early 1970, Hanshi Isaac received Black Belts in "Shotokan Karate," "Kung Fu" (Crane), the Korean Art of "Tang Soo Do," and "Shorin-Ryu." Hanshi Isaac is quoted as saying, "what I have found is that all Okinawa Karate is actually 'Uchinandi' or 'Okinawa-Te." Regardless of what style of Okinawa Karate one studies, practices, or trains in, it will fall into one of the 3 original forms (styles)--Shuri-Te, Naha-Te, or Tomari-Te.

Over the years there have been a number of styles brought to Okinawa by the various services, from Taekwondo to Budokai Jujitsu, that is not Uchinadi. Even after 35 plus years, Hanshi Isaac feels he is only taking "baby steps." Competing in well over 700 tournaments in a 16-year span (prior to retiring from the tournament circuit about 8 years ago), winning well over 2000 trophies, being inducted in 17 Halls of Fame, having studies under three (3) living Okinawan Grandmasters--Hanshi Isaac states that "every time I think I've learned something, I find out how much I don't know. The learning never ends."

Whenever old Martial Arts is spoken in America (USA), legendary Marines, fighters like Mr. Don Nagel, Joe Lewis, Don Bohan, Gary Alexander (1st American Karate Champion), the "old student Bill Hayes (author and historian and Total Martial Artist), and the "young student" Doug Perry (who gives a new meaning to the word "Hard") come to mind. Modern America often speaks of Jujitsu and

Judo, but one of the greatest is Mr. Ernie Gates and Mr. E. L. Mayfield ("Dr. Death" as he was called in the old days), and Major Drexel Heard, one of the best total Martial Artists in the world--you name it, he can do it. Professor Ernie Gates is a retired Marine, 5 time all Marine Judo Champion, 1st Non-Japanes to ever win the Ambassador's Cup from Japan in Judo, one of only a few to be awarded Professorship in Judo, and 3-time winner of the Colonel Biddle Award, which is the Oscar of Judo.

Hanshi Isaac has been blessed over the years by being named 5 times as National Champion, and 3 times as World Champion. In fact, there is a little bit of Marine Corps history that few people know about. The founder and developer of the Marine Corps L.I.N.E. System of Hand-To-Hand Combat, M/Sgt. Ronald Donvito, and current Marine Corps Martial Arts Program Developer, M/GySgt. Cardo Urso, are both Hanshi Isaac Black Belts. Already the debate stirs about which is better. Everything has a past, a present and a future. Regardless of the opinions, we must always remember, just as with the clock, the car, and the airplane, someone or somebody started it and others have taken the ball and worked to make it better. Time tests everything and for servicemen and servicewomen, the battleground is our best teacher. What is important is that two Marines were called upon and they both accomplished the Mission: Hand-To-Hand Combat and a Martial Arts Program.

George Jackson

"Sifu Jackson met many great masters who taught him the intricacies of their craft..."

Studying martial arts made a tremendous impact on Sifu Jackson's life. It had a positive impact on students at all levels and gave him the confidence to perform at a high level in various aspects of law enforcement. He met many great masters who taught him the intricacies of their craft. He's traveled and has been exposed to other cultures and enforcement at a high level. Sifu Jackson met many great masters who taught many finer points about their art.

BIO

In 1962, while assigned as a Security Forces member of the 6th Combat Defense Squadron (SAC), Walker AFB, New Mexico (NM). Sifu Jackson received self-defense, which members of the base judo team taught. Sifu Jackson joined the Walker AFB Judo team and competed in numerous tournaments around the U.S. That year, he won his first major tournament with the 15th Air Force as a white belt.

TRAINING INFORMATION

- Martial Arts Styles & Rank: Grand Master, under the American Kajukembo Association (AKA), 2nd Degree Black Belt in Kodokan Judo, 1st Degree, Black Belt in Shotokan Karate, and 1st Degree Brown Belt in Aikido
- Instructors/Influencers: GGM Richard Parelta, Alii Don Nahoolewa, Kodokan Judo Institute, All Japan Karate Association, Japan Police Academy, Waseda University, Torride High School Kendo Program, Master Yamaguchi's, (The Cat) Dojo, Inokuma Sensei
- Birthdate: December 6, 1944
- Birthplace/Growing Up: Gadsden, AL
- Yrs. In the Martial Arts: 59 years
- Yrs. Instructing: 56 years
- Instructor

PROFESSIONAL ORGANIZATIONS

- AKA
- Federal Law Enforcement Organization
- AFOSI Retired Agents Association

PROFESSIONAL ORGANIZATIONS

- Fraternal Order of Police
- California Narcotics Officer Association
- Veteran of Foreign Wars
- American Legion

PERSONAL ACHIEVEMENTS

- Degree in Criminal Justice
- Certified FLETC instructor, Agent of the Year
- Many other military awards
- Radio and TV personality in Alabama, New Mexico and Puerto Rico

MAJOR ACHIEVEMENTS

- Private Pilot Dignitary Protection Agent, UC Agent
- Tournament champion in judo and karate at various tournaments
- Responsible for schools around the globe as a result of his teachings

Donald Jett

"Studying Martial Arts gave the external and internal foundation of life and sharing culture to make a difference ..."

BIO

It was in 1968 that I discovered Chinese Martial Arts. Playful as I was and seeing Kung- Fu movies, my father put me in the care of a Taiwanese Soldier, which gave me the first introduction. As a precocious child, as recalled by older siblings, people saw me as shy and self-preserved but energetic. Any kind of disturbance, I would seem to disappear into a room and listen to Asian music. Being the youngest, if I was being picked on, my older brother told me that he would beat me up and the other person if I were beaten up. That fear alone turned me into a fighter.

First, at hand, I would like to give honor and respect to Grandmaster Ron Van Clief, who has set a path and platform for other martial artists to follow. He has given me great inspiration in my years of practice. He has a phenomenal story that surpasses many during his era and now. I remember watching his many films and as a strong

TRAINING INFORMATION

- Martial Arts Styles & Rank: Northern and Southern Chinese Martial Arts, Kenpo Karate, Shotokan Karate, Long Xing Pai (Long Hsing Dragon), Pai Lum (White Dragon), Yong Chun (Wing Chun), Ca Li Fu (Choy Li Fut), Chen Wu style Tai-Chi and Baguazhang
- Instructors/Influencers: Grandmaster Anthony Goh, Grandmaster Wang Jurong, Grandmaster Johnny Lee, Master Charles Dixon, Grandmaster Alex, Tat Mau Wong, Grandmaster Shawn Liu
- Birthdate: April 14, 1964
- Birthplace/Growing Up: El Paso, TX
- Yrs. In the Martial Arts: 53 years
- Yrs. Instructing: 40 years
- School owner, Manager & Instructor, Department of Justice Instructor

PROFESSIONAL ORGANIZATIONS

- A.C.E. Certificate
- National Organization Black Law Enforcement Executive
- Justice By Action
- Kung Fu Federation

figure as a child. He persevered in his struggle and overcame the many obstacles that came his way. Along with all the other pioneers I looked upon, you were among the best! Thank you, Ron Van Clief, for all you contributed to all martial artists alike.

PERSONAL ACHIEVEMENTS

- We are all loved first. To be positive is to know yourself and the creator. A good leader is acquired when you know yourself no matter what you do in life. If you don't know yourself, you are never going to appreciate anything in life.
- Today's work of a great human being is to know yourself and assist others. I have discovered this self -help through personal experience and dedicated learning. It's the greatest help to a given task. It seems there is no end to this ongoing process. Remember to stay positive is to enjoy yourself, plan, and accomplish with gratitude. Staying positive is the greatest personal achievement for me and others.

MAJOR ACHIEVEMENTS

- A martial artist is a human being first, just as nationalities have nothing to do with one's humanity, so they have nothing to do with martial arts. Life is a constant process of relating. So, this formed some major achievements in my life. In America, many students are taught to defend themselves from bullies at school or to feel more confident while out at night. Others belong to karate or dojo clubs and follow the tournament circuit collecting as many trophies as their talents can win.
- I wanted to learn the seemingly complex philosophical concepts or constraints with ethical notoriety from past warrior societies. The Martial way taught me technical proficiency and the external reward of athletic success. It opened the door to a rich heritage of ethical principles, training approaches, and esoteric capability that enriched my martial arts experience. It sharpened the ability to defend myself or succeed in competition, but most importantly, it is a way of living. It's the holistic discipline aimed at the pursuit of excellence, not just in the training hall but in life. I strived to apply the way in every vocation adept to achieve every field of my endeavor. This set a foundation for some major achievements like working with the Department of Justice, Big Brothers Mentoring Program, Eastern Band of Cherokee Youth programs, and many martial art awards. I owned and operated a health and wellness center and a fitness center. I organized the Art of War and China Comes to Atlanta (China Cultural Arts Festival and Expo 2003), which brought various cultures and masters from the Globe. I've officiated many tournaments, including the Battle of Atlanta and International Chinese Martial Art Championships, for many years. I thought a career in corporate law was my answer, but I turned into an Instructor with D.O.J., which opened doors to give back to society and bring cultures together; it was a great achievement.

Pat Johnson

Grand Master Pat Johnson has made such an impact in so many lives that you can't even count them", said PKA President and Battle of Atlanta founder Joe Corley.

Most people will recognize first his genius for creating fight scenes in films grossing more than a billion dollars. It was Master Johnson who created the great action in Karate Kid I, II, III and IV, Ninja Turtles I, II and III, Mortal Kombat, Batman and Robin and so many more. Prior to that, he had been the chief instructor and general manager in Chuck Norris' chain of studios in the Los Angeles area where he worked with Chuck in developing one of the greatest teams of fighters the world has ever known. "Master Johnson set a standard in the Chuck Norris studios that became a model for instructors around the country", Joe Corley said. "When Master Norris invited me first to California to train, he introduced me to Master Johnson who became my mentor, instructor, Big Brother for life. I witnessed first-hand how he handled everyone from the little kids in his Sherman Oaks school to the top-rated instructors in the world to private students like Steve McQueen and the heads of major studios to visiting instructors from around the world. His patience and guidance are without peer, and every life he touched was improved. From where did this ability to guide and influence come?

Pat Johnson was born in Niagara Falls, New York. He was raised in in a low-income area where he learned his scrappy fighting style and at the same time learned to appreciate the sincere love of a hard -working mom and nurturing family values. He also learned his strong work ethic, determination and drive here.

He began training in traditional Korean Tang Soo Do Moo Duk Kwan in 1963, while stationed in South Korea as a chaplain in the U.S. Army. While under the tutelage of a Korean master named Kang Lo Hee, Johnson earned his black belt in just thirteen months. After his army service ended, Johnson met and formed an association with Tang Soo Do instructor Chuck Norris. Johnson soon rose to the rank of chief instructor at Norris' school in Sherman Oaks, California in 1968. That same year, he formulated a penalty-point system still used by many karate tournaments.

In 1973, Norris founded the National Tang Soo Do Congress (NTC), and named Johnson as executive vice president and chief of instruction. In 1979, Norris disbanded the NTC and formed the United Fighting Arts Federation (UFAF), again naming Johnson as executive vice president.

In 1973, Pat Johnson also crafted the Tournament of Champions idea that Joe Corley implemented at the 1973 Battle of Atlanta, propelling the Battle of Atlanta into national prominence. Master Johnson brought Chuck Norris, Bob Wall, Mike Stone and Tadashi Yamashita as officials with him, setting the stage for top notch officiating at the Battle of Atlanta for many years to come.

In 1980, Johnson had a small supporting role in the feature film The Little Dragons (later known as The Karate Kids U.S.A.). In the film, Johnson played the karate instructor to a pair of young brothers

(portrayed by Chris and Pat Petersen) who use their martial arts skills to foil a kidnapping plot.

In 1986, Johnson was promoted to ninth-degree black belt. Today he is a Grand Master, a mentor extraordinaire to all he encounters and in high demand for seminars across the globe.

He lives with his wife Sue Johnson in the Valley of Los Angeles. They have four kids and two granddaughters, Lilly and Jolina Felix.

Pat Johnson with private student and friend Steve McQueen (RIP), Chuck Norris and

At Battle of Atlanta Centurion Awards Gathering, Pat Johnson with Jeff Smith, Bill Wallace and Joe Lewis

Dr. Philip Lee

"After teaching over 4000 students over the past 46 years, I can't think of anything I had rather be doing..."

BIO

My Dad had to protect himself one day and I saw him apply his martial arts skills to a group of three men and it was over in a few seconds. I wanted to be like him. That is what got me into Martial Arts. He trained me until he died, leaving me at the age of nine, with my interests at an all-time high. I kept going, but that was why I started in the first place.

I was quite shy when I was a kid. My interest in any type of martial art grew from wanting to have more and more training. I began training at my first official school when I was seventeen, having previously worked in the back yard with my cousin. When I got to that official school, my personality started to get stronger. I began to go to the front of the class, I began to make more noise than anyone else. I was chosen to be the assistant instructor. I was getting more and more confident. I started doing public speaking in college. My self-assurance was incredible. I began to compete in tournaments.

TRAINING INFORMATION

- Martial Arts Styles & Rank: Grand Master/Art of Fluid Adaption, Tae kwon Do 7th Dan, Hapkido 2nd Dan, PaSaRyu 3rdDan, Kenpo 1st Dan, Shotokan (Brown Belt) Tang Soo Do (Blue Belt), Hungar Kung Fu (Blue Sash), Muy Thai (3 years training), Krav Maga (8 years)
- Instructors/Influencers: H.P.LEE, Dan Smith, Stan Wigginton, Kang Rhee, Dale Hertzfield, Skip Beard, Benny Green, Bob Kendall, H. Tillman, Ken Eubanks
- Birthdate: September 11, 1952
- Birthplace/Growing Up: Selmer, TN / Michie, TN
- Yrs. In the Martial Arts: 59 years
- Yrs. Instructing: 50 years
- School Owner

PROFESSIONAL ORGANIZATIONS

- PKA Worldwide
- World Black Belt Bureau
- Black Belt Schools International

At one point, I was on stage performing a kata in front of five thousand people. So how has it had an impact? As a shy kid, performing in front of 5,000 people forced me to make a complete 180-degree turn to become better at everything! Now after teaching over 4000 students over the past 46 years, I can't think of anything I had rather be doing. A great friend of mine, Ken Eubanks told me that if you love what you are doing you would never work a day in your life. I now understand what he meant!

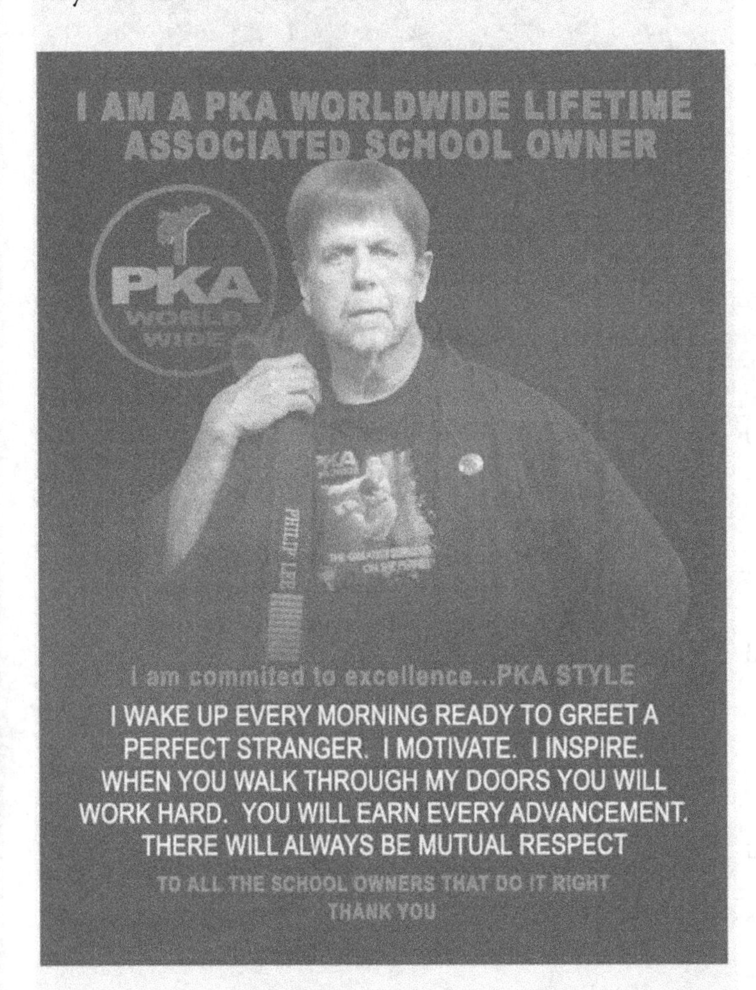

PROFESSIONAL ORGANIZATIONS

- The Alliance
- US Head of Family Martial Arts Association
- RSKC
- NASKA
- SEKAA

PERSONAL ACHIEVEMENTS

- I graduated college in 1974, I opened up my first in business in 1974, I got married in 1976 and produced two amazing sons, I kept my business going for 15 years. In 1996 I met a very independent woman who became my wife of 22 years. She is my friend and business partner .We have raised our daughter ,and now 2 grandkids. I am very lucky to have such a great group of family to be around. So, thanks to my wife Rhonda, my two sons Chris and Jesse, my daughter Lauren, my three grandkids Ally, Lilly, and Raelyn.

MAJOR ACHIEVEMENTS

- 1973 opened my first commercial karate studio
- 1978 had 4 commercial schools
- 1990 -my first year promoting an open karate tournament
- 2000 I was awarded 5-star diamond with United Professionals
- 2007 Martial Artist of the Year/Alliance
- 2009 Instructor of the Year/Alliance,2009 I received my Doctorate in Martial Arts Science.
- 2009 I was acknowledged as the founder of the art of fluid adaption/or "The Fluid Adaptive System" by 3 different Martial Arts Organizations.
- 2010 US Martial Arts Hall of Fame/Tae Kwon Do Master
- 2012 I received my 10th Dan/Grandmaster/Soke
- 2018 became a member Black Belt Schools International
- 2019 joined PKA
- 2019 I got inducted into the Martial Arts Masters & Pioneers Book
- 2020 became a lifetime member of PKA Worldwide

Eric Lee

"Martial Arts has had a major impact on my life mainly in self-fulfillment..."

I started in the Martial Arts as a family tradition, self-defense, and healing arts. Martial Arts has had a major impact on my life mainly in self-fulfillment, have self-control, focus on having a positive attitude and outlook on everyday life, to be inspired, and inspire others before I expire.

BIO

Eric Lee was born in Canton, China. His father studied martial arts, and Eric would watch him train, which inspired Eric at the early age of three. Eric later began his formal martial arts training under Chung Ball and ultimately with Grandmaster Al Dacascos. Eric was blessed to study with some of the very best martial artists in the world.

Master Eric Lee trained in both Northern and Southern Shaolin Kungfu. He excelled in martial arts and is credited with winning more national and international awards than any other martial artist in the United States. He has

TRAINING INFORMATION

- Martial Arts Styles & Rank: Wun Hop Kuen Do – 7th Degree, Kajukenbo – 9th Degree, Jun Fan Gung Fu – Jeet Kune Do, A.G. Matrix System, Northern Shaolin System, Chi Kung Meditation, Tai Chi, Proficient in over 40 Martial Arts Weapons, Expert in Multiple Martial Arts weapons training, Dao-In, Chin-Na, Grappling, and Judo, Masters Degree in Reiki, Youth and Vitality and other healing arts
- Instructors/Influencers: Grandmaster Al Dacascos, Grandmaster Share K. Lew, Master Wen Mei Yu, James Lee
- Birthdate: July 30, 1946
- Birthplace/Growing Up: Canton, China - Hong Kong, Central America Canada, Oakland & Los Angeles
- Yrs. In the Martial Arts: 50+ years
- Yrs. Instructing: 50+ years
- Manager & Instructor

PROFESSIONAL ORGANIZATIONS

- Member of the WHKD Association
- Vice President of World Martial Arts Masters Hall of Fame

been featured in almost every martial arts magazine in the world.

After retiring from competition as a 9th degree black belt, Under A. Emperado, Grand Master Lee continues to distinguish himself in martial arts instruction and the entertainment industry. He also carries on the tradition of his family and his 94-year-old father by teaching Chinese Health exercises. Has 40 Black Belts under him. Grandmaster Lee has a wide range of experience, technical expertise, and a profound understanding of various us martial arts disciplines.

Entertainment Industry Background:

- Studied with notable acting coaches
- Produced full length feature film
- Taught Seminars: How to Break into Movies Movie Stunt Fighting with Cynthia Rothrock and Art Camacho
- Studied Filmmaking and Film
- Directing Produced 40 videotapes

Author of 4 books:

- The Journey of an Artist (published by Amazon)
- 3 Sectional Staff
- The Broadsword
- Fight Back – Your Guide to Self-Defense

Travel Host: Host of the annual Eric Lee China & Hawaii Tour – since 2005

PERSONAL ACHIEVEMENTS

- Own Clothing Line -Dragon Jacket
- Movie Producer /Actor/Choreographer
- Tournament Promoter
- Teacher of Movie Stunt Fighting at UCLA
- Author of 4 Books
- Multiple Hall of Fame Awards
- 50 Magazine Covers
- Calligrapher/ Art -Oil Painting
- 40 Black Belts Under me

MAJOR ACHIEVEMENTS

- Co-Promoter – Coliseum Martial Arts EXPO and World Tournament
- 25-time Black Belt & Martial Arts Hall of Fame Honoree
- 2-time recipient of the Lifetime Achievement Award
- 2 Golden Fist Awards – (Best Weapons Champion, Best Forms Champion)
- Undisputed "King of Kata"
- Founding co-member of World Black belt, along with notable martial artists such as Chuck Norris and Bob Wall
- Winner of over 100 world titles
- Undefeated forms and weapons champion from 1970 to 1974
- Recipient of the Armed Forces Appreciation Award

Favorite Training/Hobbies/Interests:

Martial Arts, Acrobatics, Swimming, Horseback Riding, Dancing, Movies, Comedy, Singing, Hosting Dim Sum lunch parties for friends, Music of all kinds from rock & roll to country & flamenco, 1960's – involved in hot rods, attained degree in Automotive Mechanics

Grandmaster Eric Lee is passionate about life and the martial arts. He is always adding to his achievements as he learns new knowledge and increases his current knowledge and skills. His goal is to continue to grow as a person while maintaining a life of balance.

MAJOR ACHIEVEMENTS

- Innovator and Certified Trainer of the flight attendant anti-terrorist training school (America in Defense)
- Actor and fight choreographer in over 150 movies and TV productions
- Las Vegas Legacy Award Winner
- Produced a feature motion picture
- Taught Movie Action at UCLA
- Southern California Motion Picture Council Golden Halo Award Winner
- Over 50 years of martial arts experience
- Author of many martial arts instructional books and over 40 magazine covers/training videos

Gary Lee

MAJOR ACHIEVEMENTS

- Gran, Hawaiian Kosho Ryu Kenpo Jiu-Jitsu
- International Black Belt Hall of Fame
- Top Weapons in Texas, 1980
- Top Ten Fighters in Texas, 1979-1999
- Rated by Karate Illustrated Magazine, rated National
- Who's Who in Karate, 1982
- 3rd Degree Black Belt Test, 1982, Lama Nationals, Chicago IL
- Creator Six Flags Amusement Park Shows, Gary Lee's Texas Karate All-Stars,
- 1984-1994, {5,000 shows}
- Texas State B.A.S.S Federation Champion, 1987
- Filmed SIDEKICKS the movie, 1990
- Gold Medalist USAKF Nationals, Dallas, Texas, 1992
- Won five {5} National NBL TITLES, Atlantic City, NJ, 1992
- Sabaki Ryu Challenge 3rd Place Kumite, Honolulu, Hawaii, 1992
- National Black Belt League World Champion, Breaking, New Orleans, USA, 1993
- Man, of the Year, Bushshiban 1993
- BIG BASS TOURNAMENT, Sam Rayburn, Jasper, Texas, 2nd Place, 3,200.00 winnings, earned a 3rd round seed into the Classic Championship 1993, Yeah Baby!!!!
- Texas NBL Arbitrator
- Star of Hollywood Stunt Show, Astroworld, Six Flags, Houston, Texas, USA, 1993
- Creator 'KIDS EXPO" Astrodome, Houston Texas.1993-1996
- Golden Greek Top Texas Overall Winner, AOK RATINGS, 1997, 1998

TRAINING INFORMATION

- Belt Ranks & Martial Arts Styles: 9th Degree Black Belt, Okinawa Karate
- Birthdate: 1954
- Birthplace/Growing Up: Honolulu, HI

MAJOR ACHIEVEMENTS

- Nominated Black Belt Magazine "Player of the Year", 1997
- Texas Sport Karate Player, MVP
- Opened World Championship Karate Studios, 1998
- Created the Living Legends Celebrity Roast; 1999 - present.
- To date Professor Lee has celebrated 15 American Pioneers in Sport Karate.
- Staff Writer for WORLD BLACKBELT, 1999
- Created Tales OF the Old Sensei for World Black Belt, monthly column
- Master of Ceremonies, Martial Art History Museum, Las Vegas, Nevada, 1999
- Director Michael Matsuda says 'Gary Lee is the voice of Karate, Black Belt Magazine
- Director of Junior World Black Belt Kids Club
- Produced and Directed Living Legends, 'the Tim Kirby Celebrity Roast, Houston, Texas, USA, 2000
- Kumite International Black Belt Hall of Fame Award and Scholarship given in Professor Gary Lee's name for $1,000.00, Pittsburg, Pa, 2000
- Creator of BLACK BELT TV, A online network for Martial Artist and Martial arts Exclusive personal interviews with the stars of martial arts.

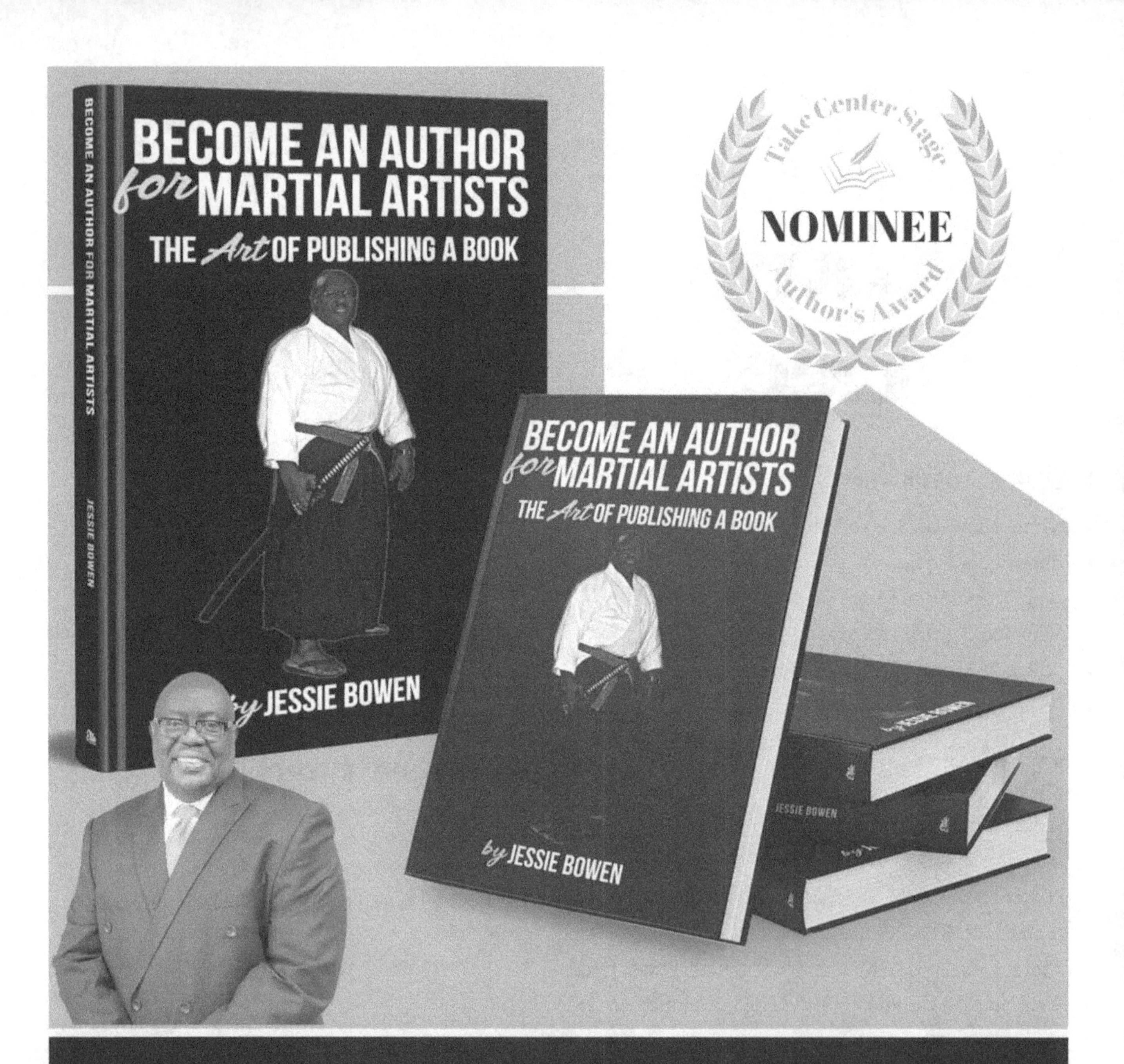
BECOME AN AUTHOR
for MARTIAL ARTISTS
THE Art OF PUBLISHING A BOOK
by JESSIE BOWEN
Take Center Stage
NOMINEE
Author's Award

Halbert Lee

"Studying martial arts over these years has taught me to be strong and confident."

BIO

When I was five years old, I saw my uncle Calvin teaching my cousin, Willie, martial arts. Then I became very interested in it. What also motivated me, at a very young age, was the unfortunate experience I had being bullied.

Studying martial arts over these years has taught me to be strong and confident. Furthermore, the martial arts has literally saved my life.

PROFESSIONAL ORGANIZATIONS

- Former member of Eastern U.S.A. International Martial Arts Association, Inc.

PERSONAL ACHIEVEMENTS

- I am an eight-time Grand Champion in kata and weapons divisions.

MAJOR ACHIEVEMENTS

- Two times inducted into Action Magazine Hall of Fame. I was also a recipient of Eastern U.S.A. International Martial Arts Association, Inc. Hall of Fame. The Harlem Goju Association Major Leon Wallace Hall of Fame Award was presented to me in May of 2019.

TRAINING INFORMATION

- Martial Arts Styles & Rank: Young Fu Pa Gar, Sijo
- Instructors/Influencers: Sifu Lu Young
- Birthdate: April 26, 1955
- Birthplace/Growing Up: New York City, NY
- Yrs. In the Martial Arts: 61 years
- Yrs. Instructing: 53 years
- Sijo, Founder & Creator of my own martial arts system

Sheldon Marr

"Having had the opportunity to coach all these great athletes has impacted my life more than anything else!"

BIO

My father, Walter (Wally) Marr, was a Black Belt in Judo and an Air Force Sgt., and he began teaching my sister and me Judo when I was five years old.

I wasn't very good & therefore didn't like Judo very much. But by the time I was 9, I had gained a little coordination and became more successful in sports. By the time I was 13, I was a State Champion and competed nationally and Judo became a huge part of my life!

I began wrestling when I was 14 years old. I used Judo against my wrestling opponents and wrestling against my Judo opponents, and I became very successful in both sports!

By the end of my junior year of high school, I was competing nationally (and internationally) in both sports, and I felt virtually unbeatable in my age group. Then I broke my neck!

TRAINING INFORMATION

- Martial Arts Styles & Rank: Grappling - 10X U.S. World Team Coach; Judo - 6th Dan; Pankration - 7th Dan; Pancrase MMA - 7th Dan; Kodenkan Jiu Jitsu - 5th Dan; Shingitai Jiu Jitsu - 5th Dan; Combat Sambo - 4th Dan; Tae Kwon Do - 4th Dan
- Instructors/Influencers: Wally Marr, Charlie Lee, Willy Cahill, Wally Jay
- Birthdate: November 24, 1958
- Birthplace/Growing Up: Huntingdon, England / Northern CA
- Yrs. In the Martial Arts: 57 years
- Yrs. Instructing: 39 years
- School owner & Instructor at Edge MMA & Fitness

PROFESSIONAL ORGANIZATIONS

- USA Grappling
- USA Wrestling
- USA Judo
- U.S. Judo Association
- U.S.A. Federation of Pankration Athlima

After breaking my neck, the doctor told me to never do Judo or wrestle again. I kinda' listened; I became a coach! I began coaching high school wrestling the following year (at the age of 18). I coached Highlands H.S. in Sacramento. The previous year, Highlands had a 0-12 record in their league. My first year there we were 5-7, & second year we were 7-5!

But I really missed competing in Judo, & I still felt I had a chance of making the Olympic Team. So, I put my coaching on hold and started competing again. Although I never felt like I really got my timing back, I did well enough in competition to make the Judo Team at the U.S. Olympic Training Center in Colorado Springs, CO. So, as soon as I graduated from college, I moved to the OTC!

After a 4-year layoff (and a fused spine), I was definitely an underdog to make the Olympic Team, but things got worse as I was ALWAYS injured while training at the OTC. I tore both shoulders, tore one of my knees & had major back problems. Then, leading up to the final Olympic Trials in 1984, my arm started going numb in practice (complications from my broken neck), and the USOC banned me from all further competition (that they sanctioned) and I had to retire again!

I started coaching wrestling again at Cherry Creek H.S. in 1985. We took 3rd as a team at the CO State Championships in '86 & '87, 4th in '88, 2nd in '89 & '90, & '1st in '91!

I started with the Denver Sheriff Dept. in 1992 and was

PERSONAL ACHIEVEMENTS

- California State Freestyle Wrestling Champion
- California State Judo Champion
- U.S. National Jr. Judo Champion/Finalist
- U.S. National Sr. Judo Champion/Finalist
- U.S. National Masters Judo Champion/Finalist
- U.S. National Collegiate Judo Champion/Finalist
- U.S. National Masters Jiu Jitsu Champion

MAJOR ACHIEVEMENTS

- Developed the Budo Kai Goju system
- Rated 4th in the fighting regional ratings in Karate Illustrated
- Rated as the world 7th contender in semi contact fighting and as the world 10th middleweight contender in full contact fighting in the World Journal Ratings
- Was the only middleweight fighter to knock down Bill Superfoot Wallace for an eight count in our contest in Denver, Colorado

their Defensive Tactics Instructor from 1994 until 2018. I opened Grappler's Edge (now Edge MMA) in 1994 and we've won 25 National Team Titles in Grappling & Jiu Jitsu since then!

I've coached the United States World Grappling Team ten times since 2007, and the United States World Pankration Team three times since 2000.

Having had the opportunity to coach all these great athletes has impacted my life more than anything else!

Vic Moore

"Martial Arts helped me develop into a better person and gave me more discipline."

BIO

I watched the Ku Klux Klan ban black folks and I wanted to be able to protect myself. Martial Arts looked like a lot of fun. Hard work, but a lot of fun. I wanted to be a world champion.

The Martial Arts helped me develop into a better person and gave me more discipline. It made me have more determination. I succeeded in football, track, and national championship teams. I ran the winning touchdown in an all-state championship, and also ran in a championship. I was on a gymnastics team that went all state. We had three teams that won state championships: football, track and gymnastics.

TRAINING INFORMATION

- Belt Ranks & Martial Arts Styles: 10th Degree Black Belt
- Instructors/Influencers: Ron Williams, Bill Demetri, Robert Trias, Mhung gi
- Birthdate: August 23, 1943
- Birthplace/Growing Up: Indianapolis, IN/ Cincinnati, OH
- Yrs. In the Martial Arts: 71 years
- Yrs. Instructing: 61 years
- School owner & Instructor

PROFESSIONAL ORGANIZATIONS

- United States Karate Association
- Traditional World Karate Association
- Black Dragon Fighting Association

PERSONAL ACHIEVEMENTS

- 1965- Beat Mike Foster and became the first grand national champion in the world. Mike Foster was undefeated, USKA Grand national in Miami FL.
- 1967- Defeated Bruce Lee in a match of speed at the internationals in California
- 1968- Defeated Joe Lewis to become the first world pro champion

MAJOR ACHIEVEMENTS

- 1966- Defeated the all Hawaiian champion for the world championship
- 1967- Defeated Chuck Norris at the internationals in California.
- 1969- Defeated Jim Kelley at the team championships. Also defeated my idol, Mike Stone who was undefeated with 91 straight victories, for the light heavyweight champion of the world
- 1970- Defeated Superfoot Bill Wallace for the USKA World Championship in San Antonio Texas
- 1975- first person to train a chimpanzee to do karate and went to tournaments

Sijo Steve Muhammad

> "Martial arts has brought me discipline, order, and control in my science for fighting."

I got a job at a Chinese restaurant, and they started teaching me Tai Chi. They used it as a form of exercise. I continued for five years; not knowing it was a fighting science. Martial arts has brought me discipline, order, and control in my science for fighting. It has allowed me to live by four Laws for Life: Spiritual Law, Dietary Law, Fitness Law, and Income Producing Law

BIO

10th degree Black Belt, Grandmaster Steve Muhammad, is a co-founder of the Black Karate Federation and the organization's first President. He is also one of the most dynamic and celebrated figures in the history of American martial arts. From his days as a tournament competitor with an unrivaled championship record, to becoming a trainer of fighting champions and thousands of martial art practitioners worldwide, Steve Muhammad exemplifies the true spirit of the martial arts tradition. In short, he is a warrior and a true gentleman.

TRAINING INFORMATION

- Martial Arts Styles & Rank: Sijo, which means founder and creator of my own science, 10th Degree Black Belt
- Instructors/Influencers: Danny Inasonto and Chuck Sullivan
- Birthdate: July 2, 1939
- Birthplace/Growing Up: MS / Topeka, KS
- Yrs. In the Martial Arts: 64 years
- Yrs. Instructing: 64 years
- School owner, Manager & Instructor at Karate of the Gods

PROFESSIONAL ORGANIZATIONS

- Black Karate Federation

Born in Topeka, Kansas, in 1944 as Steve Sanders, he was the youngest of several siblings, all of whom were raised in a tight-knit and fairly athletic family. Steve's first exposure to the fighting arts actually began observing his mother! To keep her boys in line, she developed "a mean right hook."

In high school, Steve became an outstanding athlete who excelled in football, baseball, and track. He later attended Kansas State University on a football scholarship before leaving to join the Marine Corps. While in the military as a member of the Pathfinders, he received his first real exposure to the martial arts. Training with the Pathfinders was similar to training with the Green Berets – it was intense and highly disciplined.

During his military years, Steve was stationed at Camp Pendleton, which is in Southern California. Twice a week he drove north to Los Angeles to train in Kenpo with Ed Parker. Even after he was later transferred to El Toro Marine Base, he continued to travel and train in Los Angeles. Steve's training was eventually interrupted with a tour of duty in Vietnam. The experience of fighting in Vietnam gave him discipline and a first-hand look at the reality and brutal effectiveness of combat.

After his enlistment was over in 1963, Steve returned to California and immersed himself in the study of Kenpo with Ed Parker. He earned his first Black Belt three years later under Parker's instructors Dan Inosanto and Chuck Sullivan.

PERSONAL ACHIEVEMENTS

- Founder and creator of my own science: Ken Wing Tai Ba

MAJOR ACHIEVEMENTS

- Received the title Sijo from the Asian community in 2006. Which means founder and creator of a complete science.

BIO (continued)

As a tournament competitor, Steve became a member of the West Coast Karate Team. During those early days of sport karate, he faced renowned fighters such as Joe Lewis, Al Dacascos, Chuck Norris, and Benny Urquidez. Many tournament veterans called Steve Sanders 'The fastest hands in karate.' He later received the ultimate tribute from the late Bruce Lee, who said Steve Sanders had the 'fastest hands I had ever seen.'

In the decades following Steve's magnificent tournament career, he became interested in developing a more personal approach to fighting and began to introduce his own techniques in his training. Some of his theories, such as "Brain Sight" and the "Principles of Mathematical Fighting" have revolutionized his art.

The quiet-spoken Muhammad has twice been awarded the Golden Fist Award by his colleagues, and he has been nominated for the Black Belt magazine Hall of Fame for his outstanding contributions to the martial arts. He is co-author of "Championship Kenpo," "The God Side Of Kenpo" and "Brain Sight."

In 1984, Steve Sanders joined the Nation of Islam and changed his last name to Muhammad. He later converted to Islam.

Steve Muhammad has also found time to appear in films. His most notable role was in Enter The Dragon (1973). In this classic Bruce Lee movie, Muhammad played the role of Jim Kelly's instructor. Additionally, Steve Muhammad has worked with actor Wesley Snipes for several years as his bodyguard and accompanied him throughout his film career.

Source:

USADojo.com

https://www.usadojo.com/steve-muhammad/

Jae Mun

"Martial Arts allowed me to meet many excellent martial artists while also giving me the confidence to know that I can defend myself!"

Martial arts has helped me maintain my physical health. It has helped me obtain a job now that I hold the position of President of the All-American Tae Kwon Do Federation. It has allowed me to meet many excellent martial artists while also giving me the confidence to know that I can defend myself.

BIO

I was fascinated with the jump spinning hook kick performed by my childhood friend Jong Woo only to discover it was Tae Kwon Do. South Korea was very poor at the time during the '60s. I had many hobbies; fishing at Han River, hunting with a slingshot, and ice skating at the field during winter. I joined the baseball team at my elementary school- Gang Nam, but took Tae Kwon Do lessons outside of school at the neighborhood's Do Jang (Tae Kwon Do School).

The self-defense aspect appealed to me since there were some fights at school, and there were neighborhood

TRAINING INFORMATION

- Martial Arts Styles & Rank: IJTF - International Jung Tong Tae Kwon Do 9th Dan; Black Belt World - 6 Dan- WTF; World Combat Arts Federation 6th Degree Black Belt; World Black Belt Bureau 5th Dan; Kukkiwon World Tae Kwon Do 4th Dan. ITF International Tae Kwon Do Federation 1st Dan (1975)
- Instructors/Influencers: Kong Young Il , Kong Young Bo, Al Pigeon, Sang Ki Eun
- Birthdate: June 17, 1959
- Birthplace/Growing Up: Seoul Korea
- Yrs. In the Martial Arts: 50 years
- Yrs. Instructing: 20 years
- School owner

PROFESSIONAL ORGANIZATIONS

- Alumni Westminster Theological Seminary
- Korean Pastors
- Kentucky Colonel
- Ordained Minister of the Gospel through Kosin Presbyterian Denomination

gangs. I studied during the '70s in Baltimore. Practicing self-defense was exciting. A dozen kids surrounded me with axes at a golf course and by gangs outside of a memorial baseball stadium. It helped me make new friends and build my reputation at school as a karate kid. I had a smooth school life, unlike other Asian kids who got bullied at school. I did demonstrations at Junior and Senior High, so everyone at school knew I did Tae Kwon Do. At the time, kids knew it as Karate and gave me respect or were at least wise enough not to pick a fight.

I liked competing in tournaments. It gave me purpose, took my mind off my worries, and I wanted to make my dad proud. I also continued because I liked my instructor, Al Pigeon, who led me to Christ and socializing with members after class by going to Friendly's Ice cream. I chose Tae Kwon Do, even though I made a Varsity Soccer Team in High School. I thought I would have a better chance of getting a job during my college years as an instructor. My investment in training in Tae Kwon Do paid off working as a General Manager for four years in Maryland, only to heed to my calling as a minister of the Gospel, pursuing a Master's of Divinity at Westminster Theological Seminary in Pennsylvania. I was able to work full time as a program director for many Tae Kwon Do Schools, helping them to succeed in member enrollment, then eventually becoming President of All American Tae Kwon Do Academy. I enjoy Tae Kwon Do; I use it to do ministry and help develop future leaders in America.

PERSONAL ACHIEVEMENTS

- Masters of Divinity from Westminster Theological Seminary in PA
- Youth pastor for 20 years at numerous Korean churches (AK, WA, DC, MD, and PA)
- I prepared and led short term missions to Mexico and Peru
- I helped prepare the 1980 Worldwide Evangelization Crusade in South Korea- International affairs
- Interpreter and guide to Dr. Bill Bright, Founder of Campus Crusade for Christ
- Seminar speaker for SFC
- Four-year Senator Scholarship-MD
- BS for Philosophy & Religious Studies at Towson State University

MAJOR ACHIEVEMENTS

- Masters of Divinity from Westminster Theological Seminary (2001)
- Ordained Minister of Gospel (2002)
- Promoted 9th Dan by IJTF (2018)
- Hall of Fame- Grandmaster of the year by United States Kido Federation 2-time award recipient for the spreading and contribution of Tae Kwon Do by Jun Lee President of Black Belt World (2018 and 2019)
- Hall of Fame - Evangelist/Instructor of AFKA- American Freestyle Karate Association
- Head instructor-New Life Black Belt Academy

John Natividad

Tang Soo Do practitioner John Natividad was a world-rated karate fighter before his retirement from competition in 1975. He appeared in the Top 10 polls of such publications as Black Belt and Professional Karate. His biggest year was 1973, when he won grand championship titles at the International Championships, the Colorado State Championships, Yamashita Open, Northern California Karate Championships and first places at the Las Vegas Nationals and the Black Belt Team Championships in Washington, D.C. He also owns first-place and grand championship trophies from the '72 Western States Championships, '72 Las Vegas Nationals, '71 Four Seasons, '71 Pasadena Open, '72 Pacific Coast Team Invitational, '71 California State Team Championships, '71 Four Seasons Fall Team Championships, '70 International Team Championships, and the 1970 Mike Stone All-Star Team championships in California where he burst into the national spotlight by defeating the top 5 National ranked competitors, most notable were Whirlwind Fred Wren, Victor Moore from New York, and Joe Lewis. That night earned him the title of "Giant Killer". He finished second in the heavyweight division of the World Pro/Am in '70, second in middleweight at the '72 Top 10 Nationals in St. Louis and '72 Grand Nationals in Albuquerque.

John was a member of Chuck Norris' Championship team with Bob Alegria, Victor Guerrerao, Ralph Alegria and Dennis Young, which fought all over the United States and went undefeated for 7 years.

This team fought the Japanese karate team lead by Halliburton in San Jose California and also fought and defeated the Jhoon Rhee team lead by Jeff Smith in Washington, DC.

JOHN NATIVIDAD VS BENNY URQUIDEZ

Many of us remember the 1973 fight between John Natividad and Benny "The Jet" Urquidez. It was one of the greatest non-contact bouts in history at the famous finals of Ed Parker's Long Beach Internationals where Natividad beat Urquidez 13-12 in overtime using a technique that Benny had taught him two weeks earlier. At that point in time most of the top fighters were part of Southern California Professional Karate Association under Mike Stone and they trained and fought each other, exchanging ideas and often using each other's techniques against each other.

Born in Hawaii just outside of Honolulu of Chinese and Filipino decent, John went to Germany at the age of 14 with his father, during his father's tenure in the service. After returning from traveling and studying in Europe, at the age of nineteen, John began studying Tang Soo Do with Chuck Norris, and received his black belt from Mr. Norris in 1970.

John was part of the movie documentary New Gladiators financed by Elvis Presley. The film follows a team of five American fighters who took on the challenge of the best karate fighters in the world. The film was shot over a year and a half period. Team members included John Natividad, Darnell Garcia, Tom Kelly, Ron Marchini and Benny Urquidez. Ed Parker, Elvis' instructor, and George Waite, a well-known karate practitioner, entrepreneur, and friend of Elvis's, led this team. The team traveled to England, Belgium and Germany competing.

John received the Golden Fist Award, known as Karate's answer to the Oscar, given by Mike Stone, for Best Offensive Fighter and Technician from 1972 to 1974.

He has been inducted into the INTERNATIONAL KARATE AND KICKBOXING HALL OF FAME and the MASTERS HALL OF FAME.

In the early eighties, John took over Chuck Norris' second school in Redondo Beach. This is the school where all the champions had trained. He opened a second school in Culver City where he worked with Gang members in an attempt to give them an alternative to the gangs. Then John moved to Las Vegas to finish his education, delving into pre-law. There he opened another school and called it John Natividad's World Class Karate and Kickboxing Association and to this day that name is used by his schools. In a 1990 issue of Black Belt Magazine, Chuck Norris choose John Natividad as one of the top 20 Fighters in his United Fighting Arts Federation. John has affiliate schools in northern and southern California and he continues giving martial arts seminars and teaching private lessons.

Aaron Norris

Aaron Norris said "Whoa, the stories I can tell!" as he and Joe Corley started to catch up on the last 5 decades and the great successes of the Norris Brothers. Master Corley had always marveled at the love and affection of the brothers Norris and the incredible family built by and around them, from films and TV to UFAF, KickStart and beyond.

A Stephen Covey Seven Habits principle built on synergy is at the center of these successes. Many strong people working together can produce the best forms of synergy, and Aaron Norris, is and has been, one of the key linchpins.

Some background, important to know: Aaron Norris was a 17-year-old, 150-pound, all-state (California) standout linebacker. Linebacker. The college coaches said, "Put on more muscle and come back to see us!" For those that do not know, linebackers see things differently than other players and other people. Much differently.

> "We look so forward to sharing with the world at large the incredible influence that we martial artists have had on our society and the culture, and there are so many incredible stories to tell!"

This linebacker promptly enlisted in the Army in the Vietnam era, and a year later he was a solid 200 pound "linebacker", but was now vying for an even more challenging position as a "door gunner" on a Huey (helicopter), wanting to hang at the door with a 23 pound M-60 machine gun. "Sadly, they told me I didn't have the mechanical abilities for the job I wanted, so I was trained for other challenging jobs and extended my enlistment another year."

After Advanced Infantry Training, Aaron was specially chosen to train in the Army's Non-Commission Officers Academy. He was chosen because of his leadership abilities, and his rise in rank was fast. Aaron became a Sergeant E-5 in less than a year after joining the Army--and was only 18 years old.

His older brother Wieland had also joined the Army not long after Aaron, and Wieland ended up in Vietnam. Sadly, Wieland was killed in action saving his squad and was awarded the Silver Star for bravery.

Aaron's final year found him on the "Demilitarized Zone" (DMZ), a sergeant in Korea, responsible for a platoon, with bullets flying through the zone. His service period ended shortly thereafter.

Aaron returned to California to the world of film and television. He applied his Norris family values, linebacker attitude and champion martial arts determination that led to the successes an informed observer would expect. Just some of Aaron's feature film directorial credits include Braddock: Missing in Action III, Platoon Leader, Delta Force II, Hitman, Sidekicks, Hellbound, Top Dog and Forest Warrior. Aaron also directed the critically acclaimed two-hour pilot Sons of Thunder" for CBS which was so well received that the network placed an order for six additional episodes.

Before Aaron started directing films, he wrote and produced Silent Rage, Lone Wolf McQuade and Invasion: U.S.A. He then tried his hand at acting, starring in the HBO production Overkill. He executive-produced and co-wrote Logan's War: Bound by Honor, a Movie of the Week for the CBS television network. He also executive-produced two President's Man, part of CBS' Movies of the Week franchise.

A most important historic factoid. With his brother as Walker and Aaron as the "Show Runner / Executive Producer" starting the second season, Walker Texas Ranger became a Top Ten weekly program for CBS, almost unheard of for a weekend show when homes using television were traditionally way down. Walker ran for 9 seasons and 203 episodes!

And today? It is reported that 1,000,000,000 (one billion) people a day watch Walker, Texas Ranger all over the world! Aaron's website at AaronNorris.com overflows with credits, so many credits.

Aaron is the co-founder of the "ActionFest Film Festival". His partner, Bill Banowsky (CEO Magnolia Pictures), and Aaron have built a successful franchise in the film festival marketplace.

Aaron owned the film distribution company Tanglewood Entertainment for a number of years during which time he produced and oversaw worldwide distribution of more than a dozen feature films.

In his on-the-ground martial arts life, Aaron Norris taught in and managed Chuck Norris Studios in California. He then ventured east to Virginia Beach to teach in and manage the first Chuck Norris franchised school, a state-of-the-art facility that took martial arts instruction to the next level.

While there, Aaron expanded his competitive side and won the Four Seasons Championship in Las Vegas along with other impressive titles. He then ventured to the Battle of Atlanta in 1974, where the Tournament of Champions drew in fighters from everywhere. Aaron said this was one of his favorite competition stories and learning experiences.

Aaron had used the 1973 tournament flyer as his "vision board", inserting his name in the slot that would be the Middleweight Champ in the eliminations in order to face the seeded champions. When he arrived and saw the size of the Middleweight division, he conferred right away with his brother.

Aaron said, "Carlos (Chuck) and I looked at the incredible lineup of talent, he looked at me and he said 'Lineup last Butch (Chuck called me Butch). Chuck told me this would give me a chance to watch all these people fight so I would know what to expect from them, giving me an advantage, since none of them had seen me fight. Long story short, I remember going through 12 bouts that day to win the Battle of Atlanta Middleweight Championship, giving me a slot against the 11 seeded champions. They teased me for "being so tired!" And even though I ended up losing to Fred Wren in the Tournament of Champions that day, everyone at the Battle of Atlanta knew I could fight AND could take shots from Fred Wren!". Joe Corley explained, "Everyone gained much respect for Aaron that day as 'not just another pretty face'!"

Fast forward to today, and you see martial artist Aaron Norris as the Chief Executive officer (CEO) of United Fighting Arts Federation, a 10th Degree Black Belt and a man still busy in Film and Television. "We are so proud of all our UFAF members and very excited about our new Affiliate Member program."

The Film/TV Producer/Director Aaron Norris has a mind exploding with exciting projects. "We look so forward to sharing with the world at large the incredible influence that we martial artists have had on our society and the culture, and there are so many incredible stories to tell!"

The Norris brother Aaron is equally moved by his activities in TAPS: Tragedy Assistance Program for Survivors helps the families who have lost loved ones in combat, something Aaron knows a lot about. "The Mission of TAPS is to provide comfort, care and resources to all those grieving the death of a military loved one.

Since 1994, TAPS has provided comfort and hope 24/7 through a national peer support network and connection to grief resources, all at no cost to surviving families and loved ones. I encourage all our fans to visit Taps.org to learn more and to assist", Aaron said.

Giving Back for a Lifetime. Thank you Aaron Norris. Thank you Chuck Norris. Thank you Gena Norris. Thank you to all the Norris related families for all you continue to do!

Visit AaronNorris.com for so much more…more films, video and great life adventures!

Chuck Norris

In the martial arts world, he is known by one name—Chuck.

In the film world, he is known as the nice guy who plays tough guys, and in real life is as tough as they come. And as nice. And for those in the martial arts who have worked with him these past six decades, he is known to be a giving, inspirational leader who has positively affected many millions of lives, both directly and indirectly through his chosen fields of influence.

Born Carlos Ray Norris in Ryan, Oklahoma on March 10, 1940, Chuck was the eldest of his two brothers. Chuck's brother Wieland Norris, born July 12, 1943 was KIA in Vietnam in 1970. Aaron Norris, the youngest of the three, has done everything with Chuck from producing and directing their film and television projects to serving as Chairman for United Fighting Arts Federation. The Norris family relocated to Torrance, California when Chuck was 12 years old, and he was enrolled in high school there until he graduated in the class of 1958.

Chuck Norris joined the Air Force after graduation from high school and was stationed in Korea where he was an MP (Military Police) while in the service. Chuck became a voracious martial artist. He trained every night in Tang Soo Do and spent all day Saturday and Sunday training in judo (yudo in Korea). He left Korea as Black Belt in Tang Soo Do and a brown belt in judo.

After returning to his home in California, he worked for Northrop Aviation and taught Tang Soo Do as a sideline. Just a couple of years later he had started teaching full time in his own martial arts school which not only flourished but also attracted a number of Hollywood's famous including Bob Barker from television and Steve McQueen from the movies.

TOURNAMENTS AND CHAMPIONSHIPS FOR A DECADE…

Now an international film and television star, Chuck started out as a tournament fighter. That endeavor lasted for a decade from 1964 through 1974, and it was a spectacular time for him. By 1966 he dominated the tournament scene and was almost unstoppable in competition. Fast, agile, powerful and relentless, he was in the first era of the thinking man's fighters winning over the best known fighters of the time from coast to coast.

His first major tournament victories began in 1966 with wins at both the National Karate Championships and also the All-Star Championships.

In 1967 the Norris name became well known when he won the World Middleweight Karate Championship and the All-American Karate Championship.

He set records with victories in the Ed Parker Internationals, World Professional Middleweight Karate Championship, All-American Championship, National Tournament of Champions, American Tang Soo Championship, and the North American Karate Championship, all in 1968.

Determined, handsome and polite, Norris won the admiration of his peers the hard way. Privately he was esteemed as a man who was respected and envied in the ring, who loved "his Mom's apple pie" and who loved to fight. And he did it well. He compiled a fight record of 65-5 with victories over all other champions of the day, and retired as undefeated Professional Full-Contact Middleweight Champion in 1974.

In his own words, Chuck tells us, "Whatever luck I had, I made. I was never a natural athlete, but I paid my dues in sweat and concentration and took the time necessary to learn karate and become world champion."

Toward the end of his career as a fighter/competitor Chuck was a welcomed personality and friend to several of the country's major point and professional karate tournaments including one of the most prestigious events of the time, the Battle of Atlanta. Chuck attended many of the milestone events at the Battle of Atlanta, including the Professional Karate Association (PKA) events staged in Battle of Atlanta finals. Norris and company consisted of martial arts celebrities Pat Johnson, Bob Wall, Mike Stone, Tadashi Yamashita, and Chuck's star fighter students including Darnell Garcia, Howard Jackson, Chip Wright and John Natividad. And whether running a ring as Referee or Judge or merely watching a match, the fighters stepped up their game under Chuck's scrutiny.

ACTION IN FRONT OF THE CAMERAS...

Today we know that it was Steve McQueen, one of Norris' private students who became a close friend, who urged him to try acting, and he did. It began with an uncredited part in 1968 in The Wrecking Crew, an adventure movie starring Dean Martin, Elke Somer and Sharon Tate. But Norris wasn't alone in that film. Joe Lewis, Ed Parker, and Mike Stone were also very recognizable but uncredited as was Bruce Lee, a fight and stunt advisor.

Now, over a half century later, the Chuck Norris filmography is overwhelmingly impressive. He has a star on the Hollywood Walk of Fame, well-deserved for leading roles in more than 30 motion pictures and five made-for-television movies. But even with these credits, he is likely best known to the viewing audience for his near 200 consecutive leading appearances in “Walker, Texas Ranger” as the show’s hero, Cordell Walker.

BUT NEVER REALLY RETIRED…

Retired but by no means inactive, Chuck is married to Gena O’Kelly, is a father and grand-father, and lives on a ranch in Navasota, Texas. He and his wife both serve on the board of the National Council of Bible Curriculum in Public Schools.

He and Gena are Spokespersons for the Total Gym Fitness infomercials.

Chuck and Gena, while digging for an additional water source for cattle, discovered a huge aquifer on the Norris property, and now distribute a healthy drinking water, CForce Water. (CForce Bottling Co. is a certified woman-owned business founded in 2015 by Gena and Chuck Norris. Under CEO Gena Norris’ leadership, CForce water is now available in dozens of states through thousands of retail locations. CForce is a full-service bottling facility that offers co -packing, raw bottle sales and branded product).

Chuck is also the author of five books.

He works for many charities, including the Funds for Kids, Veterans Administration National Salute to Hospitalized Veterans, the United Way, Make-a-Wish Foundation and KickStart, a nonprofit organization he created to help battle drugs and violence in schools.

He received "Veteran of the Year 2001" honor at the 6th Annual American Veteran Awards, visited US forces fighting in Iraq in

50 YEARS OF MARTIAL ARTS EXCELLENCE

November 2006, and he was made an honorary Marine in March 2007.

Chuck and his brother Aaron were made honorary Texas Rangers by Gov. Rick Perry on December 2, 2010 in Dallas, Texas.

He is a very vocal conservative Republican spokesperson and fundraiser, but has ruled out running for elected office himself, is a born again Christian, and an NRA member. In 2006 he won "The Jewish Humanitarian Man of the Year Award." In and for the martial arts...

In 2005 he founded the World Combat League, a full-contact, team-based martial arts competition.

He has founded the Chuck Norris System which he evolved from Chun Kuk Do ("The Universal Way") and American Tang Soo Do.

He has a 10th degree Black Belt in the United Fighting Arts Federation Chuck Norris System, of which he is the Founder, and also an 8th degree black belt in Tae Kwon Do. He has a 3rd degree black belt in Brazilian Jiu Jitsu (UFAF B JJ) under the Machado Brothers and holds a black belt in UFAF Krav Maga Force (KMF).

Chuck is also the Founder of Kickstart Kids, which has impacted the lives of over 100,000 students since 1990.

Paul Ortino

"The martial arts has been a blessing to me and I want to share the traditions with all who want to learn."

I wanted to help others get their self-confidence back and be able to protect themselves. I believed that every man, woman and child should learn to protect themselves and my wife Daisy, my daughters Cheryl, Sherry Anne and Shanelle all became Black Belts and helped me teach in Hawaii. My son Angelo is working his way to being a Black Belt one day. The family that trains together stays together.

BIO

I began my Martial Arts study when I was 13 in Judo because I wasn't that big and was getting into fights a lot with what we now call bullies. Wanting to be able to defend myself, I pleaded with my parents to let me take martial arts. I then started taking karate in Reading, PA and never stopped.

Everywhere I moved I signed up for Karate, Taekwondo or Kung Fu. The funny thing was that the better I got the less fights I was getting into. Having Senseis such as

TRAINING INFORMATION

- Belt Ranks & Martial Arts Styles: Hanshi,9th Degree Black Belt Okinawa Kenpo Karate Karate (GM Seikichi Odo,GM Richard Gonzalez), 9th degree black belt (GM Robert Dunn Taekwondo), 6th Dan Hawaii Karate Kodanshakai(GM Bobby Lowe,GM James Miyaji), 3rd Degree Black Belt Red Dragon Karate (GM Al Smith), 3rd Degree Black Belt Shotokan Karate, 3rd Degree Black Belt Chi lin Chuan Fa
- Instructors/Influencers: GM Seikichi Odo Okinawa Kenpo Karate (10th Dan), GM Robert Dunn Taekwondo (9th Dan), GM Al Smith Red Dragon Karate (10th Dan)
- Birthdate: July 13, 1954
- Birthplace/Growing Up: Philadelphia PA / HI, FL, NC / Las Vegas, NV
- Yrs. In the Martial Arts: 52 years
- Yrs. Instructing: 46 years
- President and Chief Instructor (Okinawa Kenpo Karate Dharma-Ryu Dojo)

Robert Dunn (Taekwondo), Al Smith (Red Dragon), Charlie Lewchalermwong (Shotokan) and finally Richard Gonzalez and Seikichi Odo (Okinawa Kenpo) I was taught the principles of Karate as well. I realized that it was better to walk away from a fight not because I was afraid of getting hurt but because I really didn't want to hurt someone else. The Martial Arts taught me to be humble, respectful and to refrain from violent behavior.

In the beginning I just wanted to protect myself but after I started training, I realized there was so much more to karate than meets the eye. It became a way of life. I no longer wanted to fight other people and was able to walk away feeling confident about myself. From the moment I entered the dojo of GM George Dillman back in the late 60's I wanted to become a Black Belt. Even before I became a Black Belt, I was an assistant instructor.

PROFESSIONAL ORGANIZATIONS

- Ryu Kyu Hon Kenpo Kobujutsu Association (BOD)
- American Martial Arts Alliance
- Hawaii Karate Kondanshakai (original member)
- Hawaii Karate Congress (former President)
- Seishinkai Karate Union (former Shibucho to Hawaii- GM Robert Burgermeister, Kaicho)
- Pennsylvania Black Belt Society
- Florida Black Belt Association

PERSONAL ACHIEVEMENTS

- Won Triple Crown -1st place kata, weapons, kumite (GM James Miyaji tournament/Waipahu HI)
- Rated in the top 10 kata, weapons and kumite in the Hawaii Karate Congress annual ratings
- Represented USA at GM Ken Funakoshi's Annual tournament San Jose CA Kumite division
- Made 4 DVDs of the Okinawa Kenpo System as taught by GM Seikichi Odo
- Martial Arts Representative for the "Strike Back Training System"
- Co-founded Florida Academy of Judo-Karate with Master Don Rosenthal 1978

MAJOR ACHIEVEMENTS

- Former President of the Hawaii Karate Congress
- Karate Commissioner for the Aloha State Games (1990-2003)
- Taught all branches of the US Military in Hawaii for 26 years
- Promoted to 9th Degree Black Belt, Hanshi June 10th 2010
- Co-founded the UNC-Greensboro Karate Club under the direction of Master Charlie Lewchalermwong 1972
- 2019- awarded " The History General Award" by Professor Gary Lee and the Sport Karate Museum

Jerry Otto

> "No matter the circumstances throughout my life, I have relied heavily on the intrinsic nature of the Bushido."

Martial Arts is the core of who I am. No matter the circumstances throughout my life, I have relied heavily on the intrinsic nature of the Bushido. The martial arts strategy and philosophy is in my everyday life, profession and relationships. To me there is no other way to live.

BIO

As a teenager, I began studying martial arts in 1965 while my stepfather was stationed in Taiwan. I practiced a local Chinese Kung Fu style in a small village on Yamingshan Mountain, outside Taipei. After returning to the United States in 1973, I began formal training in Korean Tae-Kwon Do. The following year, I undertook studies in two other styles, Okinawan Shorin-Ryu and Chinese Kempo at the Red Dragon Karate Dojo, Easton, Pennsylvania. In 1978, I received 1st Degree Black Belt. I credited Grand Master Paul Ortino, 9th Degree Grand Master of Okinawan Kenpo Karate Dharma-Ryu Dojo in Las Vegas, and Grand Master Ed Hartzell, 10th Degree Grand

TRAINING INFORMATION

- Martial Arts Styles & Rank: Okinawa Shorin-Ryu (Kobayashi), 9th Dan
- Instructors/Influencers: Grand Master Tadashi Yamashita, Grand Master Ed Hartzell, Grand Master Paul Ortino, Grand Master S.L. Martin, GM Denis Decker
- Birthdate: August 2, 1950
- Birthplace/Growing Up: Baltimore, MD, lived in Bethlehem PA USA, Taiwan, Germany, US Virgin Islands, Puerto Rico, St. Maarten, DWI, Dominica, Mauritius Island (South Indian Ocean)
- Yrs. In the Martial Arts: 50 years
- Yrs. Instructing: 45 years
- School Owner of Shen Dragon Karate Dojo

PROFESSIONAL ORGANIZATIONS

- AMAFF

Master, as being most instrumental in my early years of development.

Throughout the 70's and early 80s,' I competed in fighting, forms, and weapons, in the Regional #10 level tournaments in the Kyu and Dan ranks. I always work hard at every level to be the best I could be. My efforts were rewarded by placing in the top three places in most of the tournaments.

As a Ni-Dan in 1981, I founded The Shen Dragon Karate Dojo in Phillipsburg, New Jersey. There, I gained recognition for my teaching and quality martial arts skills. As an instructor and community leader, my efforts earned recognition in 1986 from the United States Karate Kempo Association as Teacher of the Year.

Since I was an avid regional tournament competitor in 1987, I decided to test my skills by entering my first U.S. National Karate Championship to challenge the top nationally-ranked Black Belt competitors in the United States and Canada at Master Dennis Brown's U.S. Capital Classics, in Washington, DC. At this level of competition, my debut had an unprecedented outcome, winning all the elimination rounds and finishing in a tie with Master Steven "Mad Dawg" Curran, the ranking national karate forms champion of the Senior Division. Finally, I defeated the Mad Dawg in the tie-breaking round to become the Classic's 1st Place Senior Forms Division Winner.

The success at the Washington, D.C. tournament set in motion a series of events that would raise the level of the

PERSONAL ACHIEVEMENTS

- Teacher of the Year USKKA 1986
- National Competitor of the Year USKKA 1987
- Ranked 3rd Senior Blackbelt Forms in US & Canada PKL & NASKA 1987
- Ranked 1st in U.S. & Canada in Men's Senior Blackbelt Forms NASKA 1988
- Ranked 1st in U.S. & Canada in Men's Senior Blackbelt Weapons NASKA 1988
- Ranked 1st in U.S. & Canada in Men's Senior Blackbelt Forms P.K.L. 1988
- Ranked 1st in U.S. & Canada in Men's Senior Blackbelt Weapons P.K.L. 1988
- P.K.L. "Hall of Fame" "Senior Competitor of the Year P.K.L. 1988
- Undefeated Two Division Champion Forms & Weapons
- Ranked 1st in U.S. & Canada in Men's Senior Blackbelt Forms P.K.L. 1989
- Ranked 1st in U.S. & Canada in Men's Senior Blackbelt Weapons P.K.L. 1989
- Elected to Executive Committee PKL 1990-91 as Players Commissioner

competition in the 35 and older National Karate Championship Senior's Division forever. You see, the "Senior Competitors," ages 35 years and older, were not allowed to compete in the Grand Championships Finals. The belief of the tournament promoters, at that time, was that, men and women 35 and older were not skilled enough to be featured in the Super Star Grand Championship Finals. Many great senior competitors at these tournaments like Rocky DiRico, Dale Kirby, Brian Ricci, Felix Vazquez, Ron Jenkins, Steve Curran, Lou Ferrer, Dewey Earwood, to name a few. All these seniors were highly competitive. By the end of the 87-competition year, I was ranked 3rd Place in the Senior Forms Division. During the final months of 1987, we collectively lobbied the National Tournament Promoters to allow the top senior winners to compete against the other finalists.

We received great news for the new 1988 season from both the NASKA and P.K.L. promoters; they would allow the seniors to compete in all U.S. National Karate Championships in both NASKA and P.K.L. The following year, 1988, I competed in eleven combined tournaments in the North American Sport Karate Association (NASKA) and Professional Karate League (P.K.L.) events. I won 18 first places, 3-second places, and one-third place, a total of 22 competitions to earn the top ranking in the U.S. and Canada in the Senior Forms and Weapons Divisions, in both Karate Leagues. I had won four 1st Place Titles: 2 First Place Titles in the NASKA league and 2 First Place Titles in the P.K.L. League. With a

MAJOR ACHIEVEMENTS

- AMAA Who's Who "Hall of Fame" Legends in the Martial Arts 2017
- Nominated to the World Head of Family Sokeship Council 2017
- Action Karate Magazine "Hall of Honors" Golden Lifetime Achievement Award - 2018
- Joe Lewis "Eternal Warrior Award" "Battle of Atlanta 50th Anniversary" 2018
- Featured on the front page of the AMAA Martial Arts Masters & Pioneers Book – 2018
- Featured in "The World's Greatest Martial Artists, Volume 9, by Ted Gambardella.
- AMAA "Eagle Alumni Award" Who's Who in the Martial Arts – 2018
- AMAA Charter Member – Shen Dragon Karate Dojo – 2018 – 2019 - 2020
- AMAA Advisory Board Member – 2018 - 2019
- Action Karate Magazine "Hall of Honors" Esteem Martial Artist Award - 2019
- Featured on the front cover of Action Martial Arts Magazine "Hall of Honors" Who's Who Directory 2019
- Awarded AMAA "Martial Arts School of the Year" Shen Dragon Karate Dojo, Who's Who – 2019
- Featured on the front cover & in the 2020 Action Martial Arts Magazine: "Hall of Honors" World History Book and inducted into the Martial Arts "Hall of Honors."
- Featured in the 2020 American Martial Arts Alliance Foundation, Chuck Norris, Martial Arts Masters & Pioneers Biography Book
- AMAAF Ambassador for the Caribbean Island Region - 2020
- Nominated for inclusion in The Martial Arts Extraordinaire biography – 2021 – featured on front cover
- Featured on the Front Cover of The Martial Arts Extraordinaire Magazine – 2021
- The Martial Arts Extraordinaire Magazine featured the article: The Art of Survival – How the Shen Dragon survived two cat-5 hurricanes and one year of pandemic conditions
- AMMAF Board of Advisors – 2021
- AMMAF Ambassador for the Caribbean Region

lot of intense training and support from my martial arts brothers and sisters, I repeated my success with the P.K.L. in 1989, finishing the season as the "Undefeated Champion" in two divisions, Forms, and Weapons. This was an unprecedented feat in the two black belt categories I never expected. To my knowledge, not one senior competitor has equaled dual undefeated places in one season in the history of the P.K.L. or NASKA National Karate Circuits.

In all, there were six first-place national titles in two years. My accomplishments during those years gained new respect for the senior competition division. These accomplishments also made a unique distinction in the 1988 P.K.L. Blackbelt "HALL OF FAME" as the "Senior Competitor of the Year," prompting league president Glen Hart (R.I.P.) to describe, "Jerry Otto is the greatest senior competitor in weapons and forms in the history of the national pro/am circuit" (1989.)

In 1989, I became a personal student of Hanshi Tadashi Yamashita, formalizing my knowledge in the Kobayashi Shorin-ryu Karate System. In 1991, I moved to St. Croix, U.S. Virgin Islands, and opened my second Martial Arts Dojo. In 1995, during one of Master Yamashita's visits to the my Dojo, Master Yamashita promoted me to Renshi 6th degree Blackbelt's Rank.

In 1997, my life plans changed, and I began to travel to many exotic tropical locations where I worked in the construction project management profession. I lived in Puerto Rico, teaching and training in various

MAJOR ACHIEVEMENTS

- Featured Bio and on the front cover of 2021 AMMAF "Changing Lives Series" Tribute Book with Ernie Reyes
- Chosen by the World Kobudo Federation – World Martial Arts Live – as an Instructor for their Global Teaching Seminar with 41 Countries and nearly 20,000 viewers globally. One World, One Family, Bringing the World Together Again

BIO (continued)

karate dojos, and trained briefly in Aikido. In addition, I lived in St. Maarten, D.W.I., and Mauritius Island, in the South Indian Ocean. I continued practicing martial arts and studying eastern philosophy, frequently visiting Hindu Temples conversing with the Hindu Pandits to deepen my philosophical knowledge.

I returned to the Virgin Islands in 2010. In April 2013, Soke 10th Degree Grand Master, Edward J. Hartzell, promoted me to the rank of Hanshi-Dan 8th Degree Black Belt, also recognized by Grand Master Paul Ortino of the Okinawa Kenpo Karate Kobudo dharma-Ryu Dojo. In 2020, I was honored by Grand Master Ed Hartzell and promoted to Ku Dan, 9th Degree Black Belt.

On June 1st, 2017, with my wife Celine and son Bryan's assistance, we opened the New Shen Dragon Karate Dojo in St. Thomas, US Virgin Islands. In 2019, the American Martial Arts Alliance awarded the Shen Dragon the "2019 Martial Arts School of the Year". In 2018, we introduced Krav Maga training under Grand Master Toni Morrison, which continues to evolve.

BIO (continued)

We had endured two major Cat 5 hurricanes in September of 2017 and endured island-wide mass destruction with no power for four months. In 2020, we survived one year of economic demise, holding on during the worst pandemic in American history. But we never gave up and continued to push forward against all odds to become the dominant Martial Arts Training Facility in the U.S. Virgin Islands.

Steve Parks

"What use is greatness if it isn't used to bring happiness, joy, and positive change into the lives of others?"

BIO

My martial arts journey and inspiration began in 1968 with my high school friend, Rick Cooper and Korean Taekwondo, followed by training with a work associate Steve Kovacev of the Czech Republic. I then studied a short stint with Cliff Davis in Burleson TX which in the early 70's led to my lifelong American Karate family led by GGM Billy Brammer and GM Billy Smith.

From my beginning in Martial Arts, I had heard the name of "J Pat Burleson" and his name was revered around the country as one of the BEST EVER Karate Instructors. Then, during the masterful instruction of Billy Smith and Billy Brammer, I found that they were within the same lineage and under the umbrella of Mr. Burleson's Black Belts. Although I've never had the special opportunity to train directly under Grand Master Burleson, it was always obvious that he kept a constant vigil over his entire flock and I was truly honored to have been nominated by him

TRAINING INFORMATION

- Martial Arts Styles & Rank: American Karate - Honored with 10th Degree Grandmaster
- Instructors/Influencers: Grandmaster Billy Smith, Great Grandmaster Billy Bramer, GGM J Pat Burleson, GM Max Cardoza, GM John Anderson
- Birthdate: April 5, 1953
- Birthplace/Growing Up: Fort Worth / Burleson TX
- Yrs. In the Martial Arts: 53 years
- Yrs. Instructing: 40 years
- Instructor

PROFESSIONAL HONORS

- Master's Hall of Fame
- Platinum Life Continuing Leadership Award
- USA Martial Arts Hall of Fame

for the Master's Hall of Fame. Also, in 2014, I was nominated by Master Gary Lee and inducted into the USA Martial Arts Hall of Fame. I was also nominated by Grand Master Daryl Stewart for "The Universal Martial Arts Hall of Fame".

In the beginning, and in my youth, I thought that the Karate and boxing training I would undertake throughout life would give me an "edge over others". However, over time, I have realized that the training and knowledge I've received has become a "GIFT to share with others".

In each of our lives, our hopes and dreams have done their best to guide us. Although many roads were challenging, each and every one was necessary to provide us with a clear vision of our future steps. Greatness comes in all forms and shapes, and one's opportunities for greatness are not necessarily singular in their form. Those who have achieved any level of greatness in their lives have the opportunity to share their knowledge and have a significant positive impact on the lives of others. It's not just a responsibility, but an honor, to provide others with their own hopes for greatness. What use is greatness if it isn't used to bring happiness, joy, and positive change into the lives of others? To believe that our abilities or opportunities for greatness are a single entity or achievement would be shortsighted and narrow-minded, and to believe that you can only obtain one crown in life is to sell yourself short! If we don't challenge ourselves and aspire to be all that we can be, in the areas of our lives where we are so passionate, it's not just ourselves who are

PROFESSIONAL HONORS

- The Universal Martial Arts Hall of Fame
- Superior Grand Master of the Year
- Most Distinguished Grandmaster of the Year
- History General for Sport Karate Museum
- Joe Lewis Fighting Award
- Billy Brammer Natural Fighter Award
- 2016 Who's Who in the Martial Arts
- Frank Dux Fellowship Award
- Who's Who Legends Award

PERSONAL ACHIEVEMENTS

- Married to high school sweetheart, Connie for 49 years
- Blessed with two wonderful children, Laurie Parks, who is an orthodontist and a son, Steve, Jr, who is in the mortgage industry
- Three awesome grandchildren, Michael, 24, Hudson, 13 and Ashland 10.

MAJOR ACHIEVEMENTS

- Retired at an early age
- Built and managed several successful businesses
- Creator and author of 'Poetry Pals Early Literacy Center'
- Designed, developed and patented Rage Tail Lures along with other patented fishing related products
- Extensive experience in the Whitetail Hunting industry
- Currently developing a private ranch for future trophy bass fishing and whitetail hunting in West Texas
- Living the dream!

missing out on God's blessings, but everyone around us!

In fact, each of us has MANY reasons to exist and multiple purposes for living. Each of these has its own opportunities for great service to others! Very possibly, the greatest moments of our lives are not behind us, but are ahead of us. There are more children that we can kneel before, look into their eyes and help them begin their paths and visions of great things. Young parents are waiting for us to let them know that we believe in them and their dedicated efforts toward being the best father or mother they can be. This type of encouragement, as well as sharing our belief in them, strengthens their own belief system in themselves, allowing them to achieve success in a variety of areas of their lives.

"If I can first believe in my child, my child can believe in themselves." We are all little kids in big kid's clothes. God gave us the ability and passion to reach higher and achieve these successes in life for a reason; so that we can be lights to help guide those that might follow.

Doug Pierre

"Become that continual, perpetual white belt..."

Where do I begin? Before the serious study of martial arts, I was shy and an introvert. I didn't want to upset anyone or offend them, so I took a lot of verbal and sometimes physical abuse and stayed to myself a lot growing up in Harlem.

The first five years were spent in Catholic school. In the 6th year, I attended public school, then a Catholic Boys home. My mother insisted on getting a better education, but growing up in the hood, education was not the priority, so I fought. I've always been mischievous with an inquisitive mind that also got me into trouble.

Being sent to a boy's home changed my direction. I learned to live with other people, mechanical skills, technical skills, and academic skills. I participated in all types of sports. Through the study of martial arts, I have learned that none of these matters if you are not in control of your life. Most people go along with whatever is fed to them through various methods and means. Still, as a

TRAINING INFORMATION

- Martial Arts Styles & Rank: Atillo Balintawak Saavedra Eskrima – Inheritor, Modern Arnis - 8th Dan, Kali Ilustrisimo - Certified Instructor, Soul Goju - 8th Dan, Chen Wei Gun Tai Chi - Certified Sifu, Yahming Esoteric Blade Art - Full Instructor, Universal Tae Kwon Do - 3rd Dan, Amok International Blade Fighters Guild – Instructor, Myama Ryu Jujitsu (Comb. Jujitsu/judo/aikido) - 2nd Brown, Yan Ja Pei - Muay Thai, Dragon Society International - Pressure Point Student
- Instructors/Influencers: GM Remy Presas, GM Crespulo Atillo, GM "Tatay" Ilustrisimo, GM Chen Wei Gun, GM Inocencio Glaraga, GM Judah Maccabe (Aka John Powell), GM Anthony Powell, GM Tom Sotis, GM Otis Harris, GM Carter Wong, GM Tom Muncy/Rick Moneymaker
- Birthdate: August 28, 1947
- Birthplace/Growing Up: Harlem, NY / South Bronx, NY
- Yrs. In the Martial Arts: 53 years
- Yrs. Instructing: 42 years
- School Owner, Manager & Instructor at Village Mixed Martial Arts Institute

faithful follower of the way, you gain perseverance, humility, courage, and selflessness in the service of others. You learn loyalty and the development of a serious fighting spirit. I have learned and gained so much from my study of martial arts that I believe I would never have accomplished all that I have done if not for my studies.

I would truly recommend any discipline to anyone seeking a better life for themselves without fear or self-imposed restrictions. The benefits received will amaze you.

Finally, to all my brothers and sisters in the art, who have been influenced like so many of us by movies, which is how we found out about the arts generally. All too often, we only become interested in the fight scenes. What is interesting and extremely important is the philosophy of what makes a good person and student. The principles which these movies were made for were done for the people of that culture. All too often we miss these philosophical jewels in our society, culture and martial arts training. These are the tenants by which I pattern my life, training and teaching by. With that said, the bottom line is just keep studying and training from the cradle to the grave. There is so much to learn, even when age, injury have dealt you a bad hand you can always study and learn in order to continue to contribute to society.

BIO

Until the age of 10, I lived in Harlem, New York. I had a great deal of adventure growing up. It was my inquisitive nature that got me in trouble. I went to a Catholic school

PROFESSIONAL ORGANIZATIONS

- International Modern Arnis Federation
- World Balintawak Arnis/Eskrima Association
- Yahming Kali/Eskrima/Arnis Blade esoteric Arts Association
- Guangdong Wu Shu Federation
- European Sin Moo Hapkido
- W.U.K.O. (World Union of Karatedo Organization
- Amok Blade Fighters Guild
- MAGIC (Martial Arts Grandmasters International
- NBLA (New Breed life Arts Association)
- U.S. BUDO KAI KAN

PERSONAL ACHIEVEMENTS

- 2x International Gold medalist
- 6x International Silver medalist
- 7x National Gold medalist
- 5x National Silver medalist
- Being the oldest living full contact stick fighter
- Produced 3 beautiful children
- Traveled to more than 20 countries
- Wrote a book not published yet. Coming soon
- Started a new business
- Trained 5 World Champion Stick Fighters
- Note: As far as my research has shown, I am the oldest full contact fighter in the martial arts. I still fight younger competitors. The last time i fought was in Maui Hawaii 2018. I manage to get a silver medal in sticks, bronze in knife. I will fight again if it is held in the Philippines for the last time. The fire still burns bright in me

until the 5th grade. For those unfamiliar, my hands were made tough in school from the beatings measured out by the nuns.

Fighting and the desire to know how didn't start until 6th grade in a public school; this sent me to a Catholic Boys home, where I was surrounded by hundreds of boys from all over the world. I participated in every sport available, studied a number of trades, and academics were highly emphasized. One of the Jesuit brothers in charge of our cottage taught me boxing, one of my favorites.

After two years of this i went back home, we moved to the South Bronx, and boxing came in handy. I would have to fight because of my academic mindset from the boy's home. I played HS football, but when I started college, I was exposed to Judo; the seed of this journey began, I was 20. I played with this for a short time. I watched a national geographic program about Karate. I watched men in white pajamas breaking wood, stone, chopping the heads off bottles, catching live swords with their bare hands. I wanted to do and learn from that moment.

I moved to the Lower Eastside of Manhattan, known for its fierce martial arts fighters, schools, biker gangs, thugs, drug dealers, community activists, an integrated mix of cultures, and creativity. I threw myself into the art head first, and it has been a never-ending journey of self-discovery from friends from around the world. I appeared in books, magazines, movies, training world champions, became a pillar in my community, and owned my school in New York City. None of this would have happened had

MAJOR ACHIEVEMENTS

- President R.A.I.N. a consortium of homesteaders on the lower East Side (600 members)
- President F.L.O.W. (Freer Living Our Way) H.D.F.C.
- Taking over a drug infested building from drug dealers to owning it
- Owning my martial arts school in New York
- Going to India to be in a movie (Johnny 2005)
- Traveling to several countries teaching and studying
- Being featured in several books, magazine and newspaper articles
- Creating "FORCE 12" an all-women's program of self-offense STICK FIGHTING
- Appearing at the APOLLO in New York to perform Arnis for the first time with other Martial Artists
- Appearing on ABC News Day time show teaching and demonstrating Arnis in Penn Station, N.Y.

BIO (continued)

I not studied martial arts and had the privilege of studying and learning from some great martial arts masters and people.

If my life hadn't taken this winding turn, I would have missed so much. I stay in the martial arts for two great opportunities, one to help others. The other, more importantly, to continue to grow and develop as a person. Only then can I contribute to society. There is a vast amount of knowledge gained by the study of martial arts. It goes beyond basic physical things like forms training (kata's) and self-defense techniques that may never be used because most martial artists don't live in violent neighborhoods or avoid these kinds of confrontations. It is the other things for me that fascinate me to no end. It entails nutrition, pressure point science study, biology, math, politics that affect your daily life and your students, anatomy, psychology, physics, healing, plants, animals, your relationship with the planet, and the universe. I could never get bored with martial arts; there is too much to master, especially being YOURSELF.

My reasons are obvious; martial arts have enriched my life significantly. I would recommend this practice to anyone. As for me, I will be a white belt forever. Knowledge is something to pursue from the cradle to the grave and beyond. I see life as a railroad track that we ride via a train (our body, mind, and spirit). There are stops where we get off to learn things that prepare us to continue the journey along this ride. Too often, many people get off at a stop, and unfortunately, they stay there and never get back on the train of life. It would explain why people are so rigged in their thoughts. My advice to all is to get back on the train of life and live without fear.

Donald Plummer

First and foremost, I would like to thank all of the Supreme Grand Masters, Grand Masters, Masters, and Black Belts who paved the way for me and my art.

I was born in Georgetown University Hospital in 1952 and raised in Washington, DC, until I was eighteen years of age.

My first job while in elementary school was as a Paperboy with the Washington News, Washington Star, and the Washington Post. I also helped a friend distribute Jet Magazines.

While sitting on a bundle of newspapers looking through the comic strips, I saw "The Green Hornet and Kato" strip. It inspired me so much that I grabbed The Yellow Pages, and I found Kim Studios in Silver Springs, MD. I went to the school and talked with Grand Master Ki Wang Kim. He was an 8th Degree Black Belt at the time; it was sometime between 1967 and 1969. Master Kim said that I was too young to enroll and that I needed my parent's consent. So I took the contract home to my father, Mr. Leroy Plummer, where he signed the contract and paid the fees. I was around thirteen or fourteen years old and in the 7th grade.

I earned my Yellow Belt at the Kim Studio. Unfortunately, soon after earning my Yellow Belt, I could not continue attending the Kim Studio, but I continued to practice on my own. I started teaching some of my friends the techniques that I had learned, the upper block, middle block, low block, front kick, and sidekick, to improve my skills.

The Vietnam War was raging as I turned eighteen years old at the time. One day while at a neighborhood store with a friend, President Richard M. Nixon came on the air, and he said, "We need a few good men to help stop Communist aggression in Vietnam." So I told my friend, "Let's go and enlist." We got on the bus and went down to a recruiting office on Pennsylvania Avenue near The White House. It was a no-brainer for me since my brother went into the U.S. Air Force at sixteen years old with parental consent, so I enlisted in the U.S. Air Force at eighteen years old. OSI did their investigation, and I was inducted into the USAF in three days. My friend enlisted shortly after me. She joined the Navy following her brother's footsteps.

I can't remember how I got to Lakeland AFB in San Antonio, TX, but I did. Basic training is six weeks long. On the last week of basic training, my drill sergeant asked me, "What I wanted to do in the Air Force?" I said, "I wanted to rescue people." He asked me, "Can you run a mile?" I answered, "Sir. Yes, Sir." He asked, "Can you swim a mile?" I responded, "Sir. No, Sir." and then he asked me, "Can you read?" To me, that was a piece of cake, so I gladly shouted out, "Sir. Yes, Sir." He handed me a paperback book and told me to start reading. I enjoyed reading. Being a former paperboy, I was always reading something. After I read aloud for a while, he said that I would go wherever the Air Force needed me in the service of my country. I had completed my basic training with my Yellow Belt.

I did my textbook training at Sheppard AFB in TX. Then I did my PCF duty work at Castle AFB as a traffic management specialist in Merced, California. As a 10th grade dropout, I had lots of life experience but not much formal education, but I was always eager

and willing to learn. I reached the rank of Non-Commissioned Officer in less than two years. I volunteered for duty in Vietnam, but I was not chosen to go, so I was transferred to Clark AFB in the Philippines. I didn't want to sell the car that I had at Castle AFB. I remember driving from the base back home to Washington, DC, in two and a half days, quite an accomplishment for the time. After I dropped off my car in DC, I was flown directly to the Philippines. While at Clark AFB, I earned my GED. I passed all the GED requirements in five days. I met Master Instructor Ernie Escalante. He was a wonderful teacher that taught Indonesian stick fighting. After that, I joined the Ernie Wado School, where he trained me on "The Twenty-four Techniques of Stick Fighting." I earned my second Green Belt in Indonesian Stick Fighting under his watchful eyes.

Due to an on-duty injury, I was transferred from the Philippines to Andrews AFB in Maryland, where I spent three months recovering from my injuries. I was placed on temporary military disability for five years, and in 1979, I retired from the Air Force. While on military disability, I moved back to my parent's house in DC. My friend Viny Earl found out that I was a martial artist and asked me to train him. I refused at first, but he finally convinced me into training him. I taught in my house, and when he reached the rank of Yellow Belt, I told him that he needed to join a certified school if he wanted to rise through the ranks. He did, and the last time I saw Viny, he was a second-degree Black Belt. I went back to Kim Studio; by now, Grand Master Kim was a 9th Dan. I was promoted to first degree Black Belt in 1976; my father was there to see the ceremony. I was again promoted, and in 1977 I was honored with my second degree Black Belt under Grand Master Kim. I started Howard

University in 1977 as a Black Belt with tournament experience. I trained under Grand Master Kim until 1982. The same year I moved to Bridgeport, Connecticut, to live with my brother. While in New Haven, CT, I studied Subak and got an Orange Belt. When they knew that I was a fighting Black Belt, I was introduced to Timothy Shiver and worked closely with him in the 1985 Special Olympics World Games. After that, I moved to Detroit, MI, and later to Oakland, CA, where I started training again. It was no holds barred full-contact fighting. As I remember, I returned to Washington, DC, minus one of my front teeth.

After living in Washington for a while, I moved to Baltimore, MA. I started training and teaching under Grand Master Se Yong Chang USTA, who certified me as a 2nd Dan with the WTF. After that, I transferred to Copping State in Baltimore and received an AA degree with transferable military credit.

After a seven-year absence from martial arts, I moved to Fort Lauderdale, Florida, looking forward to starting my training and my lifelong dream of becoming a Master. I started searching for a suitable school to join. After much searching, I found Grand Master Francisco Loureda, 9th Dan Kukkiwon. Under his strong guidance and demanding eye, I grew through the ranks to my current ranking of 4th degree Master in WTF Olympic Style Tae Kwon Do with the US Chung Do Kwan Association. I have trained with Grand Master Francisco Loureda for nearly ten years. I currently live in Pompano Beach, Florida where I bought a home almost two years ago, I just completed turning my garage into a private martial arts studio where I can train and be in the best shape possible and continue to work on my knowledge. In the many years and the many miles that life has taken me, martial arts has been my

constant companion. Martial arts have always given me great comfort, pride, and a feeling of accomplishment that is not found in many other places.

Places that I have traveled and trained in:

Alaska, Hawaii, Guam, Okinawa, Japan, Portugal, Morocco, France

Education and Experience:

USAF 1971-1975

Retired USAF 1979

National Business School 1976-1977

Howard University 1977-1981

Walter Reed Hospital 1982

University of District of Columbia 1983

Morgan State University 1998

Copping State AA Degree 2000

Accomplishments:

1st Degree Black Belt 1976

2nd Degree Black Belt 1977

Gold Medal AAU Howard University 1980

3rd Degree Black Belt 2014

Bruce Lee Hall of Honor 2015

USFL Poomse Certificate 2016

AAU Referee for 6 years

Who's - Who Legend Award 2017

Certified 2nd Degree Black Belt 2000

Life Achievement Award 2020

Over 30 Competition Medals

1st and 2nd Degree Kukkiwon

4th Degree Master Instructor 2018 to the Present 2021

John Prevatt

"Studying the Martial Arts has taught me over the years to be humble, care about other people and to be very patient when instructing!"

BIO

In junior college I was introduced to Larry Rhineheart, a Kung Fu Instructor who taught me how to specialize in Take Downs (spinning techniques including back fist) and groin kicks which were legal at that time. I moved to Milwaukee and joined the ATA where I achieved my Black Belt.

Then I opened a martial arts studio in Merritt Island Florida under ATA and expanded into Melbourne, Fl with active testing over 250 students.

I relocated to Tampa, Fl and eventually opened 7 studios where I franchised them out to my Black Belts and they are still open. I presently operate one studio and am considering franchising this one!!

Studying the Martial Arts has taught me over the years to be humble, care about other people and to be very patient when instructing!

TRAINING INFORMATION

- Belt Ranks & Martial Arts Styes: American Karate (9th Degree), ATA Tae Kwon Do (4trh Degree)
- Instructors/Influencers: GM Soon Ho Lee ATA, GM Young Sun Seo ATA, GM Bill Clark ATA, GM Many Aggrella
- Birthdate: July 31, 1944
- Birthplace/Growing Up: Jacksonville & St. Augustine, FL
- Yrs. In the Martial Arts: 55 years
- Yrs. Instructing: 46 years
- School owner at John Prevatt Karate, John Prevatt Martial Arts USA

PROFESSIONAL ORGANIZATIONS

- Naska Fame FBBA

I also have a great respect for children and their accomplishments while watching them excel from level to level. In addition, my own life grew as a result of teaching martial arts!

PERSONAL ACHIEVEMENTS

- Ranked # 5 Lightweight Division PKA - Diamond National Winner 1992
- Naska Fighting Champion 1992, 1996 - FBBA and FAME State Champion – 2-time winner New England Championship
- 10-time US Open winner - Empire Nationals
- 2-time Champion - Blue Grass National
- 4-time Champion Capital Classic
- 2-time Champion -Denver Mile High Champion
- Battle Of Atlanta 3 times Champion
- National Karate Competition Champion 1996

MAJOR ACHIEVEMENTS

- Inducted into The World Karate Union HOF (1996) Inducted into International HOF (1998, 2006,
- 2007) Inducted into Cosmopolitan HOF (1989, 2002, 2005, 2006) President of Tae Won Do AAU
- Inducted into Universal Martial Arts HOF (2002)
- Inducted into the Outstanding Contribution (2003) Awarded Union Martial Magazines (2005 & 2006)
- Inducted Alan Goldberg The Action Martial Arts HOF (2006 & 2020)
- Inducted into Preservation of Martial Arts (2006) Ambassador to Martial Arts (2006 & 2007)
- Honored In The World of Family Sokeship Council (2006 & 2007)
- 45 years of Martial Arts Award
- Received Highest Honor Shogun Award
- Award to Undefeated US Open Champion
- USA Martial Arts HOF Pioneer Award (2016)
- Lifetime Achievement Award (2019)

Joseph Rebelo II

"Martial arts has educated me. Martial arts has enlightened me. Martial arts has made me a seeker of knowledge."

Martial Arts has become my entire life. I am passionate about the various arts! Immersing myself in learning, studying, reading, watching videos, taking notes, recording myself practicing, teaching seminars & workshops, and teaching online classes.

Martial arts has educated me. Martial arts has enlightened me. Martial arts has made me a seeker of knowledge. It has enabled me to drink from the well of wisdom. To share that Knowledge & Wisdom with all I encounter in the arts. Martial arts has given me role models who I have been blessed to know, sitting at the feet of the masters! Be teaching the martial arts and sciences: I do what I love, I love what I do & I do it for a living! How many people in life can say that?

BIO

I started in the martial arts in 1968. My dad and I were doing father-son horseplay and he hit me with a karate chop and dropped me! Instead of crying, I asked "What

TRAINING INFORMATION

- Instructors/Influencers: Fred E. Hosmer & Jim Gagnon, Ed Parker, Frank Trejo, Tony Cogliandro, Doreen Direnzo, and Joe Palanzo, Edward Jata, John Gabriel, Jack Leonardo, Robert Smith, Carlos Febres, David German, Bill Gregory, Remy Presas, Rene Navarro
- Birthdate: October 3, 1961
- Birthplace/Growing Up: New Bedford, MA
- Yrs. In the Martial Arts: 53 years
- Yrs. Instructing: 43 years
- School owner & Instructor at Rebelo's Kenpo Karate

was that?" And he told me "That is KARATE!". He then showed me 2 books he had on the subject. He told me he was studying with David Shuster at the "House of Oyama" karate dojo in New Bedford Massachusetts. At the time, no women nor children were taught there, so he taught me various aspects of the Kyokushin system.

In 1974, I started training in Kenpo Karate at one of the first United Studios of Self Defense created by Fred Villari. The studio was in Fairhaven, Massachusetts under the instruction of Fred E. Hosmer (known as Ed). I got up to my Blue Belt and went through instructor changes before closing. I found Leo Lacerte & Chris Viera who taught a hybrid kung fu style in Leo's basement. I would meet John Gabriel at European Health Spa and would train in Tae Kwon Do/Tai Chuan Tao. Met Sensei Jack Leonardo of the New Bedford Aikikai & trained in Aiki Ken & Aiki Jo. Found Shirfu Edward Jata of the Wu Tan Kung Fu tradition from Master Jason Tsou at SMU (Southeastern Massachusetts University). I reconnected with Jim Gagnon, assistant instructor at USSD & completed my Kenpo training, having him teach at Mr. Lacerte's studio. Testing for my Black Belt along with Leo in January 1983. Mr. Lacerte contacted Ed Parker later that year and I joined IKKA and worked with Mr. Parker and others in his art. After his death, I met with David German & studied his system of TAI (Transition Action Incorporated) in its various incarnations, being listed as the official historian of the style.

MARTIAL ARTS STYLES & RANKS

- 10th Degree Black Belt (Judan) & Grandmaster Title In Kempo (Kempo International Certified)
- 10th Degree Black Belt (Judan) In Nindo Ryu Kobujutsu (Title Of "Hanshi" & Kancho)
- 5th Degree Black Belt (Godan) In Karazenpo Goshinjutsu (Past MA. Co-Vice Pres)
- 5th Degree Black Belt (Godan) In Chuan Fa/Kempo (Bill Gregory's Kajukenpo-Pai Lum) [Sigung]
- 9th Degree Black Belt (Master Of The Art) In Ed Parker's American Kenpo Karate (AKWA Certified)
- 9th Degree Black Belt In David German's T.A.I. (Transitional Action Incorporated) (Kempo International Certified)
- 10th Degree Black Belt In Chinese Hawaiian Kenpo (Pesare/Cerio Lineage) IKGC Certified
- 5th Degree Black Belt (Godan) In Nindo Ryu Atemido
- 6th Degree Black Belt (Rokudan) In Nindo Ryu Goshin Jujutsu
- 6th Degree (Rokudan) In Okinawan Kempo
- 4th Degree Black Belt (Yodan) In Nindo Ryu Gendai Ninjutsu [Taijutsu]
- 7th Degree Black Belt (Shichidan) In Nindo Ryu Iaijutsu
- 1st Degree Black Belt (Yeedan) In Tai Chuan Tao
- 1st Degree Black Belt In Tae Kwon Do
- 5th Degree Black Belt (Godan) In George Elmer's American Chinese Kenpo Karate [Technical Advisor]
- 1st Degree Black Belt (Shodan) In Mark Shuey's Canemasters Curriculum
- 10th Degree/Level (Duan/Toan) Black Belt/Sash (Hei-Se) In Shao Choy Hung Kung Fu [Chin Na-5 Animal Style-Chuan Fa] [Inheritor Of Style]
- Shir Fu (Instructor) In Northern Shaolin Praying Mantis [Liu Ho {Six Harmony}, Chi Shing {Seven Star} & BA FA OR BA BU {Eight Step} Kung Fu/ Kuo Shu/Wu Shu
- (6th Level -White Dragon Kung Fu Association Certified)
- Shir Fu in Tai Chi Chuan (Wu's Short 24, Yang's Long 108, and Chen's Short 24 Forms
- Instructor in American-Filipino Arnis-Escrima-Kali Training System
- 1st Degree Black Belt in Feliciano "Kimo" Fereira's Kempo Jutsu Kai
- Honorary 1st Degree Black Belt in Raven Kenpo Jujitsu (Technical Advisor)

I have studied over 60 styles/systems of martial arts in my career, earning rank in over 22 of them. I have a 162 IQ & a photographic/photogenic memory. I am an exception to the rule. I hold rank in Chinese, Okinawan, Japanese, Korean, Filipino & American Martial Arts. I never thought I would grandmaster, master or any of the ranks & titles I now hold. I just wanted to learn and keep learning. I say "Titles are the shields of the weak. Actions are the swords of the strong!"

PROFESSIONAL ORGANIZATIONS

- Kempo International (USA Vice President)
- Nindoryu International/World Nindoryu Federation (Kancho [Division Head] Nindoryu Kobujutsu-Weaponry
- International Kenpo Council of Grandmasters (Certified 10th Degree Black Belt & Board Member)
- International Kenpo Karate Association (Member/ Certified Black Belt/Studio Owner)
- Integrated Kenpo Karate Alliance (member/ certified Black Belt/ studio owner)
- American Kenpo World Association (Certified 9th Degree Black Belt)
- Kokusai Nihon Bugei Rengokai (Board Member & Kancho-Nihon Kempo division)
- United Martial Arts Alliance International (Senior/ Technical Advisor)
- Kempo Jutsu International (Board Member)
- Al Tracy's Kenpo Yudanshakai (Black Belt Society)
- Society of Ancient Warriors
- World Combat Arts Federation (Massachusetts State Representative)
- Mo Lum Combat Arts Society
- White Dragon Kung Fu Association
- Coalition of Ancestral Martial Arts International (Massachusetts State Representative)
- Kenpo Arts Alliance (Board Member)
- International Kempo Federation (USA Northeast Regional Representative & 2021 USA Kempo Team Member)

PERSONAL ACHIEVEMENTS

- Joseph P. Rebelo II is the Senior Instructor of Rebelo's Kenpo Karate (which includes the NINDORYU FUDOSHIN KOBUKAI and the WU TANG DRAGON MASTER KUNG FU ACADEMY - Wu Tang Lung Si Gung Kung Fu Kwoon). He has been involved in and at the Martial Arts for over 53 years.
- As an instructor, Mr. Rebelo has taught for almost half a century in the Southeastern Massachusetts area. He has been the owner/operator of 5 commercial studios. In the past, he has taught countless students at the New Bedford YMCA & YWCA, The North End Youth Agency, The Faunce Corner Racquetball Club, The New Bedford Boys & Girls Club, as well as outreach classes at various locations. He has been a self-defense instructor for the New Bedford Auxiliary Police and the New Bedford Chapter of the Guardian Angels. He has instructed civic groups such as the Southeastern business women's group on his "Everyday Gestures that will save your life" lecture for practical self-defense. He has taught group and private lessons throughout his tenure, Now focusing on long-distance advanced students as well as local individuals. He is considered by many as a "Walking encyclopedia of Martial arts".
- As a tournament competitor, Mr. Rebelo was in the top ten for both KRANE (Karate Referees Association of New England) & PKL (Professional Karate League) in 1989. He was listed in "Karate Illustrated" magazine and was the first top ten rated competitor performing Mr. Parker's Forms in tournaments in New England. He has also promoted/produced 4 open tournaments in the New Bedford area.
- A noted martial arts historian, Mr. Rebelo is frequently asked for information on various arts and has been quoted in texts as well as on the internet as a valued resource on martial arts history. He has been inducted into 5 Halls of fame as a historian. He has one of the largest martial arts book, magazine and video collections in the United States. He has also been a featured TV announcer for the Ocean State Grand Nationals and the Junior National Karate Championships & co-hosted "Championship Kickboxing" in the Rhode Island area. Later, He created Television programs: "Martial Arts Today TV ", "Self Defense & You" and the self-titled "Rebelo's Kenpo Karate". Presently, He has produced over a dozen instructional DVDs on the diverse arts in which he holds rank. He has over 170 videos on his YouTube Channel. He has been featured on half a dozen various podcasts discussing his career.

MAJOR ACHIEVEMENTS

- 1989 KRANE Top Ten in Soft Style Black Belt Forms
- 1989 PKL Top Ten in Black Belt Forms for Region 12
- First black belt to be rated in New England performing Ed Parker Kenpo forms
- Member of 2021 USA Kempo Team for International Kempo Federation
- Honored by New Bedford City Council for martial arts career
- Honored by New Bedford Mayor Fred Kaliz teaching senior citizens on "World Tai Chi Day"
- Action Martial Arts Hall of Honors member "Outstanding contributions to the martial arts"
- World Martial Arts Federation Hall of Fame "Historian of the year"
- Budo International Magazine Hall of Fame-Martial Arts Historian
- Al Tracy's Kenpo Hall of Fame - inaugural member (2007) & Lifetime Achievement Award (2011)
- International Kenpo Council of Grandmasters Hall of Fame
- Been featured on half a dozen internet podcasts
- Co-Host of Alan Goldberg's "Action Martial Arts Power Hour" on Verohive and YouTube.
- Master of ceremonies for the Action Martial Arts Mega Weekend trade show @ the Tropicana in Atlantic City, New Jersey.

Walt Rodd

“Over the years I have taught over 1000 students; individual as well as multi-generational families!”

After teaching so many students, so many families over the years, I have been invited to major milestone events in their lives, graduations, weddings and other social gatherings. After all this time, Martial Arts IS my life!

BIO

A co-worker had just been promoted to First Dan Black Belt, and opened up a club in Flat Rock, Michigan. Martial Arts sounded interesting to me. I started training on November 9, 1971 under Grandmaster Jae Joon Kim, President of the Traditional Tang Soo Do Federation.

I was promoted to First Dan on March 20, 1976 by Grandmaster Jae Joon Kim.

I was promoted to Second Dan on April 23, 1978, Third Dan on December 17, 1986, Fourth Dan on April 17, 1990, Fifth Dan on March 27, 1993, Sixth Dan on September 13, 1997, Seventh Dan on January 30, 2003 all under Senior Grandmaster Jae Joon Kim.

TRAINING INFORMATION

- Martial Arts Styles & Rank: Tang Soo Do, 9th Dan
- Instructors/Influencers: Senior Grandmaster Jae Joon Kim, Senior Grandmaster James Saffold, Choung Koe Woong
- Birthdate: April 6, 1946
- Birthplace/Growing Up: Temperance & Monroe MI / Toledo, OH
- Yrs. In the Martial Arts: 50 years
- Yrs. Instructing: 50 years
- School owner at Rodd's Martial Arts

PROFESSIONAL ORGANIZATIONS

- American Kwan Tang Soo Do Federation
- World Tang Soo Do General Federation
- League of Grandmasters
- U.S. Army Veteran of the 3 Battalion, 80 Artillery, Sargent Missile Unit in Darmstadt, Germany
- American Legion
- Boy Scouts of America

After his death, I continued training under Grandmaster James Saffold. I was promoted to Eighth Dan on March 20, 2010 under Senior Grandmaster James Saffold, President of the American Kwan Tang Soo Do Federation.

In October 2017 I traveled to Seoul, Korea. There I tested and passed my Ninth Dan under Senior Grandmaster Choung Koe Woong, President of the World Tang Soo Do General Federation, on November 3, 2017.

I teach Martial Arts at the same club in Flat Rock, Michigan I started at 50 years ago. I teach Tang Soo Do, traditional forms, as well as bo staff, numchuck, and kama forms.

Over the years I have taught over 1000 students; individual as well as multi-generational families from grandparents, parents, children, grandchildren and even great grandchildren!

A number of students went into the military or law enforcement, and continued to train under me to keep sharp and in shape.

PROFESSIONAL ORGANIZATIONS

- 4H
- Retired from Ford Motor Company, 30 years at the Woodhaven, Michigan Stamping Plant
- NRA

PERSONAL & MAJOR ACHIEVEMENTS

- Achieving my Ninth Dan
- Founded and operated Rodd's Martial Arts in several locations in Southeastern Michigan and the Toledo, Ohio area
- Conducted training, promotional examinations and seminars at numerous locations in the Metropolitan Detroit, Southeastern Michigan, and Northern Ohio locations
- Judging at and supporting Tang Soo Do Tournaments in Michigan, Ohio, Florida, Pennsylvania, and Tennessee

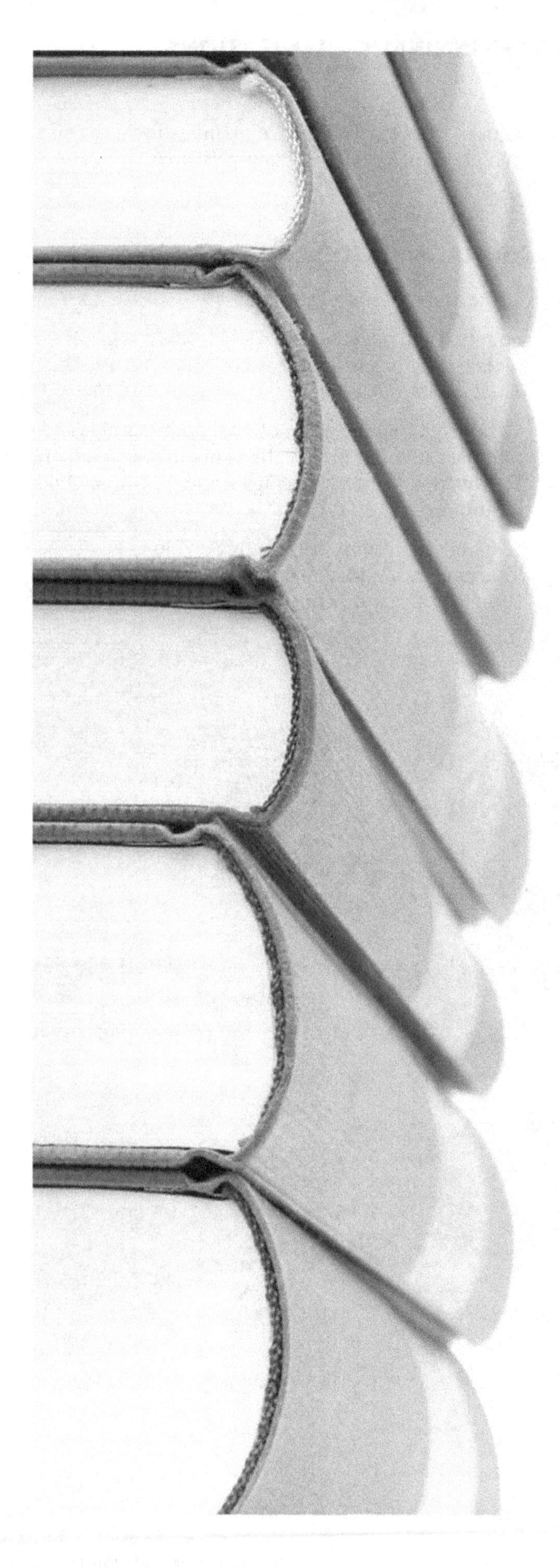

Daniel Ross

"Martial Arts has allowed me to meet and train with some of the best martial artists in the world !"

Martial arts has given me focus and helped me to find a release for anger and stress as well as allowing me to help others such as special needs children, elderly, handicapped, and at-risk youth. It has also allowed me to meet and train with some of the best martial artists in the world and discuss philosophy and history of martial arts.

BIO

I was born on January 25th, 1963 in Des Moines, Iowa. My family lived in the small farming community of Prairie City, Iowa for the first six years of my life and then, when my father got a new job, we ended up moving to the city of Des Moines. Unfortunately for us, it was a bad area we ended up moving into. Gangs, drugs, neighborhood bullies, and break-ins were common. So, my oldest brother took myself and my other brothers to the local YMCA to start studying self-defense under the Kim's Academy banner. This would begin my 49-year journey in the martial arts.

TRAINING INFORMATION

- Martial Arts Styles & Rank: Taekwondo 9th Dan; Chinese Kempo 7th Dan; Brazilian Jujitsu Brown Belt
- Instructors/Influencers: Grandmaster Yong Chin Pak, Grandmaster Angelito Barongan, Grandmaster Renner Gracie
- Birthdate: January 25, 1963
- Birthplace/Growing Up: Prairie City, IA / Des Moines, IA
- Yrs. In the Martial Arts: 52 years
- Yrs. Instructing: 35 years
- School owner, Manager & Instructor (Retired)

PERSONAL ACHIEVEMENTS

- Speaker at Pulmonary Arterial Hypertension Conference
- Governors Citation of Excellence

MAJOR ACHIEVEMENTS

- Received 3 USA Martial Arts Halls of Fame
- Action Martial Arts Magazines Hall of Fame
- Munich Hall of Honors
- Masters of Karate/Kungfu Hall of Fame
- Who's Who in Martial Arts
- Who's Who in the World Instructor of a 30-day training course for the Hillsborough County Sheriff's Office in 2016
- Teaching women's self-defense classes at colleges across the country every summer since 2014

Eugene Sedeno

> "I love sharing what I have learned and watching the faces of my students as they progress."

I have gained so much from my training. Starting in elementary school, my grades improved, my ability to analyze math problems increased and my overall outlook on learning improved. This followed me all the way to my Master's degree.

I have met so many interesting people and got to visit and teach all over the world. I love sharing what I have learned and watching the faces of my students as they progress.

I consider myself extremely fortunate to have been born and raised in Hawaii and taught by teachers who are legends. Because of them, I have been able to defend myself and my family and, more importantly, stay healthy and happy.

I owe all my success in life to my teachers, who taught me to never quit, to think, analyze and to be happy.

TRAINING INFORMATION

- Martial Arts Styles & Rank: San (3rd) DAN, Shidou-in in Okinawa Kobudo, Go (5th) DAN Kenpo Karate, IKKA, Ku (9th) DAN, Grand Master in SHAOLIN KENPO, Ku (9th) DAN, Senior Grand Master in KAJUKENBO, Ju (10th) Dan, Professor in CHINESE KEMPO, Shihan, Master of KOSHO SHOREI KENPO
- Instructors/Influencers: Shihan Mikio Nishiuchi of Kochi, Japan, SGM Edmund Parker, SGM Rick Alemany and GGM Ralph Castro, Professor Walter Godin and Sijo Adriana Emperado, Professor Walter Godin and Professor William Kwai Sun Chow, Professor James Masayoshi Mitose
- Birthdate: August 31, 1952
- Birthplace/Growing Up: Honolulu, HI / Kalihi and Waianae, HI
- Yrs. In the Martial Arts: 58 years
- Yrs. Instructing: 51 years
- School owner & Instructor at Sedeno School of Self-Defense

PROFESSIONAL ORGANIZATIONS

- American Teachers Association of Martial Arts
- Kajukenbo Self Defense Institute
- Kajukenbo Ohana Association

BIO

I was always interested in martial arts as a child. Growing up in Hawaii, I was always surrounded by them. Philippine stick fighting, Judo, boxing, Aikido, Karate, Kenpo and Kajukenbo. I have been teaching since 1969, and am currently instructing at Sedeño's School of Self Defense in Albuquerque, NM.

I started boxing and Judo with Mr. Raymond Yee at the age of ten in Kalihi Valley, Oahu. At the age of 12, when I moved to Kaimuki, I started in Kajukenbo with Professor Walter Leo Niakala Godin, a black belt of Sijo Adriano Emperado.

I stayed with him and his assistant, Mr. Tony Cambra, until we moved to Waianae in 1967. In Waianae, I started training with Mr. John Makepa and Brother Abe Kamahoahoa, students of Professor William Kwai Sun Chow. While in high school, I met Professor Rick Alemany in Waianae. I have been teaching with and for him ever since.

I received my first black belt from Grand Master Brother Abe Kamahoahoa in Waianae, Hawaii, in 1970. I also received a Black Belt from Professor Walter L. N. Godin with an extra certificate from his school at the Palama Settlement.

In 1980, I won the Chinese Martial Arts Association's and the International Kung Fu Association's Competitor of the Year Awards. My last major win, prior to retiring from competition, was at the 1984 International Karate

PROFESSIONAL ORGANIZATIONS

- International Shaolin Kenpo Association
- Okinawa Kobudo Association, USA
- Sei Kosho Shorei Kai

PERSONAL ACHIEVEMENTS

- In 1980, I won the Chinese Martial Arts Association's and the International Kung Fu Association's Competitor of the Year Awards. My last major win, prior to retiring from competition, was at the 1984 International Karate Championships, where I took first place in the Masters/Instructor Division in Kenpo Kata.

MAJOR ACHIEVEMENTS

- 2019 Portugal, Hall of Fame, Platinum Lifetime Achievement Award
- 2008 Masters Hall of Fame, Platinum Life Achievement Award
- 2007 Charter Member of Kenpo International Hall of Fame
- 2002 Masters Hall of Fame, Golden Life Achievement Award
- 1999 Recognized at Kenpo's Historic International Gathering of Eagles for contributions to the art
- 1993 Inducted into the World Martial Arts Hall of Fame as INSTRUCTOR OF THE YEAR
- 1987 Recognized in Who's Who in American Martial Arts
- 1984 Recognized in Knights of Heaven - Brotherhood of Martial Arts
- 1983 Recognized in Who's Who in Karate
- 1981 Recognized in James M. Mitoses book "What is True Self-Defense"
- 1980 Won the Chinese Martial Arts Association's and the International Kung Fu Association's COMPETITOR OF THE YEAR awards

Championships, where I took first place in the Masters/ Instructor Division in Kenpo Kata. I was also a private student of Mr. Edmund K. Parker and was promoted by him on November 20, 1980 to the rank of 5th degree Black Belt.

On May 7, 1999, the International Shaolin Kenpo Association's Great Grand Master Ralph Castro promoted me to the rank of 7th degree Black Belt with the title of Professor.

On August 18, 2005, I was promoted to the rank of 9th degree Black Belt, with the title of Grand Master, in Shaolin Kenpo by Senior Grand Master Rick Alemany.

On June 17, 1996, I was promoted by the International Okinawa Kobudo Association, USA to the rank of Sandan by Shihan Mikio Nishiuchi of Kochi, Japan.

Sijo Adriano D. Emperado promoted me to 9th degree Red Belt with Silver Trim and Grand Master in the Kajukenbo system on June 12, 2007.

I was also the last person promoted by Great Grand Master James Masayoshi Mitose, before his death twelve days later, to the rank of Master on March 15, 1981.

On November 5, 2019, I was promoted to 10th degree Black Belt in Godin's Kula Ona Kupale Chinese Kempo by Professor John Hackleman and in the presence of Professor Walter L. N. Godin's daughter, Delilah.

Pascal Serei

> "I've been sharing my expertise teaching and guiding students in their own quest for decades..."

I've been in martial arts my whole life, and it gives me respect for others, perseverance in effort, and discipline.

BIO

I started martial arts in 1957 with my father, who was a Judo and Jiu-Jitsu teacher. I always loved it and was training every day. I still train every day. To improve oneself and better oneself is a lifelong quest, you therefore can't be satisfied until you attain perfection and that does not happen. This means you always continue to train and search for the details that help you go forward. On top of the training, martial arts became a part of my identity, and I've been sharing my expertise teaching and guiding students in their own quest for decades. I was passionate about martial arts and still am.

TRAINING INFORMATION

- Martial Arts Styles & Rank: Aiki Ju-Jitsu 9th Dan, Hanshi, Ju-Jitsu 7th Dan Kyoshi, Goshin Jutsu 7th Dan, Aikibudo 5th Dan, Judo 2nd Dan, Karate 2nd Dan, Nihon Jiu-Jitsu 1st Dan, Kobudo 3rd Dan, Muay Thaï Kru
- Instructors/Influencers: Master Georges Serei, Jacques About, Master Raymond Damblant, Master Hiroshi Nakamura, Master Minoru Mochizuki, Master Yoshio Sugino, Master Goro Hatakeyama, Master Teruo Sano, Master Ari Anastasiadis, Master Alain Floquet, Adjarn Nick Hewitson, Master Hiroo Mochizuki
- Birthdate: October 15, 1953
- Birthplace/Growing Up: France / Canada
- Yrs. In the Martial Arts: 64 years
- Yrs. Instructing: 46 years
- School owner at Nintai Centre d'arts Martiaux

PERSONAL ACHIEVEMENTS

- Being a motivator, an inspiration, and a guide in life and martial arts to my students, instructors, and whoever wants to learn martial arts

MAJOR ACHIEVEMENTS

- Merit and Honor Gold Belt, Quebec, 1989
- Canadian Black Belt Hall of Fame, Canada, 2013

Mark Shuey

"The success of The Warrior Cane project has encouraged instructors to teach all over the United States."

BIO

I am humbled to have been included in articles in the media, like the article by Jennifer Levitz in the Saturday July 12, 2008 edition of The Wall Street Journal entitled "Everybody Is 'Cane Fu' Fighting At Senior Centers, So Watch Out (Older People Get Healthful Exercise And Learn to Wield a Ready Deterrent)". To be interviewed on major television sports and entertainment programs (PBS, NBC, ABC, FOX) helped to bring Mark's system of cane self-defense to the attention of the world at large.

In addition to Cane Fu, I created several other systems for the use of the cane: The American Cane System (a traditional martial arts curriculum with ranking), Cane Chi for Health and Exercise, Cane-Ja for street self-defense and the Silver Dragons for those over 50.

The Warrior Cane Project was created by Thomas Forman and Mark is a partner in this organization as an instructor

TRAINING INFORMATION

- Martial Arts Title: Grand Master
- Studied Tang Soo Do, Tae Kwon Do, and Hapkido
- Teaching for 39 years
- Started studying Martial Arts in 1970

PROFESSIONAL ORGANIZATIONS

- USMA Hall of Fame
- World Head of Family Sokeship Hall of Fame

PERSONAL ACHIEVEMENTS

- Formed the Cane Masters International Association for students of the cane and to certify instructors for his system
- Recognized in article by Jennifer Levitz in the Saturday July 12, 2008 edition of The Wall Street Journal
- Interviewed on major television sports and entertainment programs (PBS, NBC, ABC, FOX)

conducting sessions at multiple Armed Forces bases and across the country. Its purpose has been to assist wounded veterans help with rehabilitation, providing them with combat canes and training sessions for free. The success of this project has encouraged instructors to teach all over the United States and train Wounded Warriors to become Combat Cane Instructors.

MAJOR ACHIEVEMENTS

- 1970 Started Martial Arts in the Chuck Norris System of Tang Soo Do
- 1978 Received 1st degree Black Belt
- 1979 Started teaching; Master's Certification with USNKA (United States National Karate Assoc.), ATAMA (American Teacher's Assoc. of the Martial Arts), USMA (United States Martial Arts Association), and the Independent Karate School Association.
- 1994 Competitor of the year in with the National Coalition of Martial Artists.
- 1997 Rated #2 in overall points in the Pacific Rim Tour Tournament circuit.

MAJOR ACHIEVEMENTS

- Rated #1 in traditional weapons and katas in M.A.R.R.S for his age division and number #2 in overall points.
- 1998 Unified World Martial Arts Federation 1st place Forms katas, traditional weapons, kumite and won overall Grand Champion in both traditional weapons and forms.
- Grand Champion in Kata's Golden State Karate Assoc. (GSKA) as well as first place in the traditional senior weapons and open weapons, kata and kumite.
- National title in traditional senior weapons in IMAC,
- Competitor of the Year by IKSA.
- Inducted into the Martial Arts Masters, Pioneers, and Legends Hall of Fame as a "Master Instructor"
- 1999 Promoted to 7th degree by the USMA and ICHF
- NASKA'S World and National, Masters Traditional Weapons Title, IMAC'S National title
- 2000 Defended his World Champion title for NASKA and won top honors in the World for the KRANE Ratings.
- Inducted into the USMA Hall of Fame, as well as the prestigious World Head of Family Sokeship Hall of Fame.
- Formed the Cane Masters International Association for students of the cane and to certify instructors for his system.
- Recognized as a Grand Master by the World Head of Family Sokeship for the creation of the CMIA.
- 2001 Defended his National and World titles on the NASKA tournament circuit (again in 2002)
- Inducted into the Action Martial Arts Hall of Fame, International Association of Karate, Kobudo, Puerto Rico Hall of Fame and USMA.
- Appointed to the Board of the World Head of Family Sokeship.
- 2003 Inducted into the Black Belt Magazine Hall of Fame as "Weapons Instructor of the Year".
- 2008 Created Cane-Fu cane self-defense and exercise system for seniors and the physically challenged

Darrell C. Simms, Sr.

"Karate has not only been a tool for changing my life, but it has also served as a tool for empowering others."

BIO

I was introduced to the Goju (Japanese) style of Karate in 1968 by a First-Degree Black Belt Roderick Hawkins. I was so impressed with the power of martial arts, that I never missed a day of training and, if necessary, would walk to class in the rain, sleet or snow. It was this initial training that inspired me to increase my knowledge and understanding of the martial arts. At that time, Karate became a key factor in my ability to rise above the negative influences experienced by young men of color on the southside of Chicago. It became a personal tool for mental and physical development. During this period, I also had the privilege of meeting and visiting the Dojo of John Keehan (AKA Count Dante).

When Sensei Hawkins left the city, I began searching for a Dojo where I could receive comprehensive training in Karate, I discovered the JJ School of Karate, Ltd. There, I trained under Master James A. Jones and Sensei Benjamin

TRAINING INFORMATION

- Martial Arts Styles & Rank: Universal Shorei-Goju Karate System, 8th degree Black Belt
- Instructors/Influencers: Roderick Hawkins, John Keehan, Master James A. Jones, Sensei Benjamin Peacock
- Birthplace/Growing Up: Chicago, IL
- Yrs. In the Martial Arts: 53 years
- Yrs. Instructing: 45 years

PROFESSIONAL ORGANIZATIONS

- Professional Karate Commission
- Martial Arts Karate Association
- Universal Shorei-Goju Karate System
- American Martial Arts Alliance

Peacock, who was the Chief Instructor at the school. During this period, I experienced the most dramatic development as a karateka (karate student). I developed my knowledge and skills in theory, Kata, sparring, self-defense, and martial arts weaponry under the careful supervision and intensive training of Master Jones and Sensei Peacock.I won several awards and championships while attending JJ School of Karate, LtdI, including: Special Award for Outstanding Demonstration at the National Karate League Martial Arts Expo in 1975, an event that featured notable martial artists such as Jim Kelly and Ron Van Clief; and First Place in Sparring at the National Karate League Championships in 1976.

After returning from school to complete my college education, I joined Shihan Benjamin Peacock at the Three Circles School of Karate and Physical Fitness. It was there that I experienced the most extensive Black Belt training. Under Shihan Peacock, I became the Head Instructor and received the "Instructor of the Year Award" in 1992. In addition to winning several Black Belt competitions, I've taught Karate and self-defense at the City Colleges of Chicago; the Chicago Housing Authority; the South Suburban YMCA, and Governors State University. I am currently a member of the Board of Directors for the Universal Shorei-Goju Karate System, a Regional Promoter for the Professional Karate Commission and the Head Karate Instructor and Assistant Director for the Hazel Crest Park District. Throughout the years, Karate has not only been a tool for changing my life, but it has

PERSONAL ACHIEVEMENTS

- Bachelors of Science in Business Administration from Chicago State University
- Master of Business Administration from Olivet Nazarene University
- Public Administrator: City of Chicago (1984-88); Chicago Park District (1989-91);
- Metropolitan Pier & Exposition Authority (1994-98); Chicago Housing Authority (2001-05)
- Business Owner (2005-14)
- Assistant Director, Hazel Crest Park District (Present)
- President, Martial Artist Networking with Urban Professionals (MANUP)

MAJOR ACHIEVEMENTS

- National Karate League Championships
- Chicago Metro Championships
- Tri-State Championships
- AKA National Championships
- Featured in a 2010 documentary on martial arts produced by Grand Master James A. Jones Jr.

also served as a tool for empowering others. Consequently, I have created S.M.A.R.T. Fitness, a multi-purpose cardio self-defense program (www.smartfitness-chicago.com) and M.A.N.U.P, a martial arts mentoring initiative designed to empower at-risk youths with life skills and principles of martial arts that build character and integrity. These endeavors, among many other deeds and contributions, will constitute my legacy in the proud tradition of martial arts.

MAJOR ACHIEVEMENTS

- Promoter/Director: The Traditional Warrior Karate Championship and Martial Arts Exhibition
- Simms Traditional Warrior tournament videos are on YouTube
- Outstanding Demonstration Award at the National Karate League Martial Arts Expo, 1975
- Instructor of the Year (1992)
- Universal Shorei-Goju Karate System, Board of Directors
- Professional Karate Commission, Outstanding Leadership Award (2017)
- AMAA Who's Who in the Martial Arts Hall of Fame Award (2017)
- United States Martial Artist Association Hall of Fame (2018)
- American Martial Arts Alliance Eagle Award (2018)
- Action Martial Arts Magazine Hall of Honors, Esteemed Martial Artist Award (2019)

Billy Smith

"Each student, each parent of my students and all the friends I have made in the Martial Arts have pushed me to be better."

BIO

I was invited to a Karate demonstration by my good friend, Lee Delaney. The demonstration was by Great Grandmaster J. Pat Burleson. I loved it and joined that night. My friend Lee had joined the night before. Lee later went into the Army, which delayed his training. I was honored a few years later to test him for his 1st degree Black Belt. I had no idea that night of the demo would set me on a path to touch the lives of so many people.

From the very beginning, my confidence level went up. The differences in my outlook shifted as I progressed. I started meeting some of the most impressive people who had a huge impact on me. Mr. Billy Brammer taught me karate, how to be a thinker and how to be tough. More importantly, he taught me how to be a man. I did not have a father figure until he came into my life. I will be forever grateful to him. Each student, each parent of my students and all the friends I have made in the Martial Arts have pushed me to be better. I couldn't imagine my life without Martial Arts.

TRAINING INFORMATION

- Martial Arts Styles & Rank: American Karate, 10th Degree Black Belt
- Instructors/Influencers: Mr. Billy R. Brammer
- Birthdate: April 30, 1950
- Birthplace/Growing Up: Fort Worth, TX
- Yrs. In the Martial Arts: 52 years
- Yrs. Instructing: 50+ years
- School owner & Instructor

PROFESSIONAL ORGANIZATIONS

- WMARA
- Master's Hall of Fame
- USA Hall of Fame
- Universal Hall of Fame
- Who's Who

PERSONAL ACHIEVEMENTS

- It was 1970 and I was 19 years old when I started training in martial arts. I started training with Grand Master Larry Richie, who was an instructor and a student of Grand Master J. Pat Burleson. Grand Master Richie moved to Houston. I then began training with Grand Master Billy Brammer, who taught at the Fort Worth YMCA for Grand Master Burleson. I trained with Grand Master Brammer and tested for the 1st Degree Black Belt in December of 1974 under Grand Master J. Pat Burleson. In 1975, I fought for the Professional Full Contact team as a Light Heavy Weight for Grand Master Burleson. I achieved several promotions in the 70s, 80s, and 90s and was presented with my 10th degree in October of 2010. I accepted this honor from my teacher, a man who has been like a father to me, Grand Master Billy Brammer. It was such a humbling experience. I was surrounded by so many of my own students, my family and friends.
- I was honored to be inducted into the Masters Hall of Fame in 2012, the USA Hall of Fame in 2014 and the Universal Hall of Fame in 2015. I have also been honored to be included in Who's Who. I would like to point out that I have also been honored to help train and be a part of the lives of some of the most extraordinary people. I thank God every day for the help and support of some very fine Black Belts, especially Steve Parks, who has been my right-hand man for 45 years. I am so blessed and privileged to be able to do what I love to do. I have always thought that if my students and their parents appreciated what we have been able to do for them, that's enough for me.

MAJOR ACHIEVEMENTS

- I really consider my major achievements to be my personal life. I have the most incredible family and friends. They have supported me in everything I have done. I have been married to my wife, Ginger, for over 50 years and we have two beautiful and talented daughters. We have a grandson and a granddaughter, who I know are the best grandchildren ever born. All my siblings and their spouses have been the greatest throughout the years. It's still a lot of fun and so sweet. The friends I have made through karate are my best friends. I truly can't imagine not having met them and having them in my life. I have a beautiful farm that is hard work but worth every bit of blood and sweat. I'm blessed with what I think is the most wonderful life.

Clarence Smith

"The love of people has been very important in my life while learning or teaching Martial Arts."

BIO

I got started in the Martial Arts o build confidence in elementary school, and since I was one of the smallest students, I needed to learn how to defend myself. The Boys Club had a program, and I joined to keep bullies from taking my money and teasing some of my friends.

Martial arts taught me the confidence to be sure of myself and any decisions I needed to make, whether for work, family, or friends. It taught me to RESPECT everyone until they show me differently. Discipline helped me become a better leader. The love of people has been very important in my life while learning or teaching martial arts. I never knew martial arts would have such a strong impact on my life. I learned that martial arts are a lifestyle. I am blessed and thank God for leading me, the students, and my family.

TRAINING INFORMATION

- Martial Arts Styles & Ranks: American Tang Soo Do - 9th Dan (Gudan) / Chu Ida Yong Tae Kwon Do - 1st Dan, Sifu, Bai Lung Chuan Fa
- Instructors/Influencers: Grandmaster James Cummings Jr.
- Birthdate: November 8, 1957
- Birthplace/Growing Up: San Angelo, TX
- Yrs. In the Martial Arts: 54 years
- Yrs. Instructing: 44 years
- School Owner, Manager & Instructor

PROFESSIONAL ORGANIZATIONS

- VP of the Tang Soo Do Karate Association
- True Force Alliance Lifetime Member
- AOK
- UMA

PROFESSIONAL ORGANIZATIONS

- Gold Cup Circuit (California)
- Martial Arts Council of America (IMAC), Ambassador
- President/Owner of Karate For Your Body
- History General for the Sport Karate Museum Texas (2017)

PERSONAL ACHIEVEMENTS

- Four-time Instructor of the Year
- Three-time School of the Year
- 2003, 2006, 2010 Competitor of the Year
- 2017 Grandmaster of the Year
- 2017 Who's Who Legends Award
- 2017 History General Award
- 2017 Dragon Image Fighting Award
- 2018 Executive Black Belt Competitor of the Year

Inducted into the National Hall of Fame by the International Martial Arts Council in:

- 2003 – "Most Distinguished Master"
- 2007 – "Most Distinguished Grandmaster"
- 2008 – "Lifetime Membership Award"
- 2009 – "Silver Life Award"
- 2010 – "Golden Life Award"
- 2011 – "Excellence in Teaching Award"
- 2016 – "Ambassador of Martial Arts"
- 2018 – "Living Legend Award"
- While in Los Angeles, California, I taught at 5 Learning Centers, Churches for Christian Ministry, and Boys and Girls Clubs. In addition, I taught and competed with great martial artists such as Tory Russo and Master Stephanie DeLoach. I was also named to the Directorship of Southern California.
- Professionally, I've achieved an MBA in Global Business and BBA in Business Management, Blackbelt in Lean Six Sigma Methodology.

MAJOR ACHIEVEMENTS

- In 2003, inducted into the United States Martial Arts Hall of Fame/International Martial Arts Council of America (IMAC); Tested and earned my 8th degree under Dr. Dan Netherland (RIP) in 2007, Las Vegas, Nevada, earned my 9th Dan through IMAC Sr. Grandmaster Richard Bustillo as the Head Chairperson IN 2016; in 2017 was officially listed as one of the Ambassadors for IMAC, Living Legend for IMAC in (2018). Nationally ranked in the early eighties in Region Six (Texas and Louisiana) by Black Belt Magazine and Karate Illustrated with my partners Grand Masters Tom Balmos and Johnny Thompson in Kata, Kumite and pioneering the way with specialty katas.
- Developed a state-of-the-art school with outstanding black belts Grandmaster Walter Bryant, Grandmaster Clarence Bowman, Jim Ross, Master Mike Jones, Master James Smith. Darrell Dickerson, Derrick Lacy, and super students winning on the local, state, and national levels.

Irving Soto

"Seeing my students become successful in life through the study of Martial Arts practice and training is fulfilling."

BIO

I was born in the Bronx and started training in the martial arts of Jujitsu (1956) at the tender age of 2- years old. I grew up in Brooklyn, NY, a neighborhood known as Brownsville East NY. Economically, my family was very poor.

My mother had very little money to spend on any activity, but she managed to enroll me in martial arts classes held in the back of a laundromat. Once I stepped into the martial arts school, I discovered it was going to be a way of life for me.

One of my first teachers in martial arts that I trained with was O-sensei Tashioshi, who was Japanese. He taught me the application of Jujitsu. I received my black belt at the age of 11-years-old.

Tashioshi invited me to attend an international martial arts tournament held in Tokyo Japan Many years ago.

TRAINING INFORMATION

- Belt Ranks & Martial Arts Styles: Atemi Jujitsu Waza, Aiki Jujitsu (10th Degree Black Belt Founder System)
- Instructors/Influencers: O-sensei Tashioshi, Charlie Sparrow, Rudy Jones, Dr. Moses Powell, Saigon Ellis Evans, Daniyal McEaddy, Ronald Duncan, Aaron Banks, John Denora, Siegfried Boedeker, Rev. Dr. Donald Miskel
- Birthdate: March 7, 1954
- Birthplace/Growing Up: Bronx & Brooklyn, NY
- Yrs. In the Martial Arts: 65 years
- Yrs. Instructing: 57 years
- School owner, Instructor, Founder of Atemi Jujitsu Waza, Aiki Jujitsu

I was amazed by what I saw that day. O-sensei Tashioshi moved back to Japan in early 1968. I continued my thirst and quest for martial arts knowledge of Jujitsu.

I furthered my instructions with a group of masters in the neighborhoods from where I grew up in Brooklyn, New York. (1973). I was invited by the Japanese association to compete in an open championship tournament held in Japan, upon winning the Kumite. I got the opportunity to travel overseas to obtain martial arts knowledge. Throughout the years, I continue to train within the United States with other masters in martial arts.

Soke Grandmaster Irving Soto is a winner of numerous championships and the last person to be taught Atemi, Aiki jujitsu waza. He has been studying and teaching the martial arts of Atemi jujitsu waza for the last 57 years.

Soke Soto has traveled all over the world to demonstrate his Techniques and been teaching the military arm forces like the army. Soke Soto has been in numerous commercials, and tv shows such as MTV, NBC, Phil Donahue Show Live TV, Inside Edition, New York, Newsday, Barbra Sang live TV network show, The Aaron Banks live martial arts show, and the Oriental world of self-defense Show at Madison Square Garden Production. Soke Soto has been inducted into the Aaron Banks martial arts Hall of fame.

Soke Soto has appeared in GM Aaron Bank live tv show in martial arts for 47 times. He's also appeared on the live Hong Kong Television by Raymond Chow, and on sports

PROFESSIONAL ORGANIZATIONS

- Sport Karate Museum Dragon Image Fighting Award
- Samurai Ju jitsu Association international /All-Japan Sabukan Martial Arts & Way Association
- Daito-Ryu Aiki Ju- jitsu Director Association of the United States of America)
- USA Martial Arts Hall of Fame Alliance all systems
- International Martial Arts Hall of fame GGMRHF
- WOMA World Organization Of Martial Arts
- USA Warlord Martial Arts magazine
- Sekai - Day Han Martial Arts Federation
- US International Grandmasters Soke Union Worldwide
- Black Dragon Fighting society BDMFS
- Oriental World of Self-Defense Show at Madison Square Garden /Gm Aaron Banks 1960 -PRESENT
- World Professional Martial Arts Organization Gm Aaron Banks
- The Hitokui Tora Martial Arts Federation / Dr. Dan R. McEaddy
- International Martial Arts Olympic Committee Martial Arts Olympic I.M.A.O.C 01/09/2009
- America's Finest international Martial Arts Federation
- United States Head Of Family Martial Arts Association International Supreme Elite Warrior Council
- World Organizer of Martial Arts
- USA & Japan Atemi International Ju jitsu Federation

TV ESPN Sports Martial Arts Channel, the list goes on. Soke Irving Soto is an author of five books. He has been honored by former Mayor of San Diego Susan Golding and by Mayor of Hollywood Johnny Grant.

Soke Grandmaster Irving Soto is a member of the law enforcement community. He has taught special operations overseas and the United States and the federal police, New York Sheriffs' Federal Correctional Facilities and NYPD tactical defense for DEA, FBI, the US Treasury, teams for the Navy, as well as teaching for the DOD police academy and the department in Aberdeen Maryland.

Soke Soto has received accolades from former Mayor Susan Golding of San Diego, CA, former Mayor Dinkins of New York City and Mayor of Hollywood CA Johnny Grant, Brigadier General, US Army Commanding Rodger A. Nadeau, US Army Aberdeen Proving Grounds. Colonel US Army Deputy Installation Commander John T Wright for his hard work in teaching the US armed force 2002- 2016. Irving Soto is still teaching, training, and working with the military to the present day.

"As a coach in the martial arts, it's been a great fulfillment to teach martial arts science in rural neighborhoods and communities around the countryside to young men, women, kids of all ages and from all walks of life.

Seeing my students become successful in life through the study of Martial Arts practice and training is fulfilling. I enjoy working within the local neighborhood, helping

PERSONAL ACHIEVEMENTS

- Soke Grandmaster Irving Soto is a winner of numerous championships and the last person to be taught Atemi, Aiki jujitsu waza. He has been studying and teaching the martial arts of Atemi jujitsu waza for the last 57 years.
- Soke Soto has traveled all over the world to demonstrate his Techniques and been teaching the military arm forces like the army. Soke Soto has been in numerous commercials, and tv shows such as MTV, NBC, Phil Donahue Show Live TV, Inside Edition, New York, Newsday, Barbra Sang live TV network show, The Aaron Banks live martial arts show, and the Oriental world of self-defense Show at Madison Square Garden Production. Soke Soto has been inducted into the Aaron Banks martial arts Hall of fame.
- Soke Soto has appeared in GM Aaron Bank live tv show in martial arts for 47 times. He's also appeared on the live Hong Kong Television by Raymond Chow, and on sports TV ESPN Sports Martial Arts Channel, the list goes on. Soke Irving Soto is an author of five books. He has been honored by former Mayor of San Diego Susan Golding and by Mayor of Hollywood Johnny Grant.
- Soke Grandmaster Irving Soto is a member of the law enforcement community. He has taught special operations overseas and the United States and the federal police, New York Sheriffs' Federal Correctional Facilities and NYPD tactical defense for DEA, FBI, the US Treasury, teams for the Navy, as well as teaching for the DOD police academy and the department in Aberdeen Maryland.
- Soke Soto has received accolades from former Mayor Susan Golding of San Diego, CA, former Mayor Dinkins of New York City and Mayor of Hollywood CA Johnny Grant, Brigadier General, US Army Commanding Rodger A. Nadeau, US Army Aberdeen Proving Grounds. Colonel US Army Deputy Installation Commander John T Wright for his hard work in teaching the US armed force 2002- 2016. Irving Soto is still teaching, training, and working with the military to the present day.

men and women build a sense of awareness and confidence in their abilities in everyday life. I've owned my martial arts business for over 47 years and grateful to make a difference and positive influence in the community. "

Daryl Stewart

"Being introduced to the Martial Arts was probably one of the best things that ever happened to me or possibly to anyone else."

BIO

Grandmaster Daryl K. "Bigfoot" Stewart was introduced to karate by his friend Buddy Raines. They were out surfing and that day, the surf was really going off with waves crashing on to the beach. Buddy said Daryl, "Come go with me." GM Stewart said "Buddy, look at the surf, it's really good." Buddy replied, "Hey you will like it, it's about fighting." So off they went. Later, GM Stewart was introduced to a gentleman by the name of David Yeaman. He was actually introduced to karate in 1962 in Amarillo, Texas but was only there for a couple of weeks. So other than that, GM Stewart really doesn't count that in his inventory of martial arts. He says his journey in the arts started in Galveston, Texas. It turned out that he would continue to be his instructor for most of his career. He is still doing it today and has been for over 50 plus years.

Daryl was very young when he started studying Judo and Karate. He believes that the martial arts played a major

TRAINING INFORMATION

- Belt Ranks & Martial Arts Styles: 10th Dan Black Belt, Tang-So-Do, Isshinryu, Japanese styles, Korean Tae-Kwon-Do, Kung-Fu, 4th Dan in Iss-Hogai Jujitsu, 1st Dan Black Belt in Modern Arnis, 1st Dan Black Belt in Kobuko
- Instructors/Influencers: Master David Yeaman
- Birthdate: July 7, 1948
- Birthplace/Growing Up: Nixon, TX
- Yrs. In the Martial Arts: 58 years
- Yrs. Instructing: 55 years
- School owner, Manager, Instructor, Promoter

PROFESSIONAL ORGANIZATIONS

- Professional Karate Association "Lifetime Member 2020"
- Universal Martial Arts Hall of Fame "Vice President"
- Masters Hall of Fame Alumni

role in his life. The martial arts gave him a solid framework of discipline and self-confidence as he was growing up. He associated with like-minded people that had direction and helped him to stay out of trouble. While surfing and studying the martial arts, he had a framework to stay in excellent shape. At this time, he was surfing in contests for major surfing companies and traveling all over to surf in competitions in the surfing community and also at the same time entered into Karate Tournaments. He was going to school, working, training, and enjoying the life of a kid. Not knowing at the time, he was setting the path that his life would be headed down into the future.

The martial arts gave GM Stewart confidence that he could take care of himself and his mother. He and his mother lived in Galveston, Texas at the time. With his mother working long hours to support them, and single, he wanted a way to help watch over his mother. At this point, he was having a hard time with his school work and trying to make ends meet. With the guidance of his dear mother, and that of his Martial Arts instructor, Mr. David Yeaman, he moved up through the ranks in karate and judo. He was pretty much always a natural in sports so he took to karate naturally.

Being introduced to the Martial Arts was probably one of the best things that ever happened to GM Stewart or possibly to anyone else. Through the training and discipline of the Martial Arts, he has tried his best to always be kind and friendly to everyone that he meets.

PROFESSIONAL ORGANIZATIONS

- Ambassador and History General for the Museum of Sport Karate for over 23 Years
- Arbitrator for the "Texas National Tour Circuit" 1997
- Arbitrator and Judge for the National Black Belt league for the last 23 years for "The Great State of Texas"
- Judge- Amateur Organization of Karate
- Judge- Texas Karate Organization
- Judge- The United States Karate Association
- Remy Presas (IMAF) International Modern Arnis Federation
- Texas Martial Arts Hall of Fame

PERSONAL ACHIEVEMENTS

- Studying the martial arts has given GM Stewart confidence and the ability to focus on one self and others. To spread the knowledge that he has received throughout his career from other great people and the martial arts. To help them give back to our kids and adults, and our future generations. To help them prepare for their lives and help prepare other people in their pursuit of life. He always likes to say that martial arts is good for the Mind, Body, and Soul. To show them the way through knowledge of martial arts and to help keep them off the streets and out of trouble. To give them guidance and positive influences in their pursuit of happiness to keep the minds and body in shape and to give off a positive attitude. To always be helpful to others in the martial arts and the community.

To show kindness and help to any one that may require his help or that may need some guidance. To be supportive of everyone and encourage others to do the same. He does his best to help the younger generation with their lives and encourage them to strive to be a better person, to reach out in life and embrace it with zest to reach their goals. In life, if you can envision it, you can reach it if you believe in yourself. And to teach them some life skills in the Martial Arts to work on themselves to go through the belt system to prepare their minds, body and soul and achieve their goals as they go through the ranks.

The Martial Arts gave him a path to help him throughout his life to reach his goals that he has wanted to achieve. He has met many interesting people throughout his life. The Martial Arts has been the key. He has been around the world a couple of times in the Military and saw and done things a lot of people may never have the opportunity to do. He thanks God for taking care of him along the way in his travels. He always strives to be a better person every day.

MAJOR ACHIEVEMENTS

- Coach and fighter for the United States Navy Seabees Fighting Team 1972-1975
- Induction into "The Universal Martial Arts Hall of Fame" in 2000 Houston, Texas
- Induction into "United State Hall of Fame" 2001 Oklahoma City, Oklahoma
- Induction into the "Action Martial Arts Magazine Hall of Fame" in 2001-2002 Atlantic City, New Jersey
- Induction into the "World Christian Martial Arts Hall of Fame" 2001 Newark, New Jersey

Johnny Thompson

> "Grand Master Thompson is surrounded by a myriad of great blackbelts who have made him what he is today."

Receiving the bulk of his expertise from his deceased Senior Grand Master James Cummings Jr., Grand Master Thompson is surrounded by a myriad of great blackbelts who have made him what he is today. He owes it all to his family of TKA blackbelts. The dedication, loyalty and professionalism that they possess are shown in the students that they teach, who admire, respect and follow their every direction. All of this goes to show that, to date, the Tang Soo Do Karate Association has promoted 167 quality blackbelts.

BIO

I began judo in Germany during grade school and high school, and it was a difficult time because my mother was German, which was my first language, and my father was in the United States Air Force in Texas. Many people were drawn to me because of the way I spoke and dressed, and I fought every day because I lacked skills at the time. Then, I found a recreation center after school one day and

TRAINING INFORMATION

- Martial Arts Styles & Rank: 9th Dan (Gudan), 1st Dan in Chu Ida Yong TaeKwonDo, Sifu ranking in Bai Lung Chuan Fa
- Instructors/Influencers: Sr. GM James Cummings Jr.
- Birthdate: September 8, 1958
- Birthplace/Growing Up: Chateauroux, France / Germany
- Yrs. In the Martial Arts: 50 years
- Yrs. Instructing: 50+ years
- School owner, Manager & Instructor, Full-time Consultant

PROFESSIONAL ORGANIZATIONS

- United States Air Force, Retired
- Harley Owners Group (Alamo Chapter), Sergeant at Arms

spent many a night scrubbing and washing mats just so I could earn some time to get taught. They helped create the confidence I needed to go forward with my martial arts career.

With over 50 years of martial arts experience and teaching, over 40 of those years included being nationally ranked in Region Six by Black Belt magazine and Karate Illustrated with his partners Grand Masters Tom Balmos and Clarence "Daddy-O" Smith in kata, kumite, and specialty katas back in the early eighties, he has spent his life helping and mentoring all who have crossed his path. Coming out of retirement back in 2001, he competed in Kata and Kumite in the Executive Master's division and swept the competition, winning at the completion of the year at the UMA circuit end of year banquet, receiving the Grandmaster of the Year award. He has been forced to retire due to physical limitations.

PERSONAL ACHIEVEMENTS

- Martial Arts Title and Styles: American Tang Soo Do - 9th Dan (Gudan) / Chu Ida Yong Tae Kwon Do - 1st Dan, Sifu, Bai Lung Chuan Fa
- Instructor: Grandmaster James Cummings (Retired Army, Deceased 2003)
- Teaching for over 43 years
- Began studying Martial Arts in1971 (50 years in June 2021)
- Inducted into Master's Hall of Fame in 2016 in San Antonio, TX
- Member of Dr. Ted Gambordella's Martial Arts Masters Association Lifetime Member
- Professional Organizations include: President, Tang Soo Do Karate Association (TKA), True Force Alliance Lifetime Member, AKBBA, PKA, UMA (at one time), WBBB, International Martial Arts Council of America (IMAC) Ambassador, History General for the Sport Karate Museum Texas (2017)
- AMAAF Martial Arts Ambassador of the Year 2020 (Grand Master Jessie Bowen)

MAJOR ACHIEVEMENTS

- Watching all the major achievements that martial arts has given me and, in turn, what it has done for our students and blackbelts, is all worth it while working on the full circle system. I have received much more from them than I could ever believe and have been fortunate to have been able to have a full career in the United States Air Force while traveling and still teaching all over the world.
- A certified Police Instructor who is certified in the training of the ASP baton & various other enforcement tools such as handcuffing, pepper spray usage and handgun retention. He has taught, trained and certified many commissioned security officers in the State of Texas. He is also a certified Fugitive Recovery Agent, a commissioned concealed weapons owner and teaches several courses pertaining to Bail Enforcement and is the owner and operator of Technical and Tactical Security Consultants and J & L Trophies, now retired.
- Grand Master Thompson, along with GM Tom Balmos, was a successful promoter of the Annual Battle of the Alamo Open Karate Championships in San Antonio, where he was also a board member of the United Martial Arts (UMA) organization. A respected member and Ambassador of the International Martial Arts Council of America (IMAC).

Theodore Vick

"I believe I got started in martial arts to help people and show them a better way to live mentally and physically."

Martial arts have impacted my life in various ways; such an increased knowledge of dealing with people inside and outside the arts. I started teaching many kids what I had learned. I believe I got started in martial arts to help people and show them a better way to live mentally and physically. My thought process is diplomatic and open and has put me in the position to be recognized in books and magazines; I even wrote an article for Action Martial Arts Magazine in 2008. I've also received many awards and recognitions from my peers. My greatest achievement was receiving the 50 years of Dedication Award from Action Martial Arts Magazine in 2020. I received this award in front of a huge audience with my family and close friends present. This award truly signifies the impact I have made to the Martial Arts and the impact it has made on me. Martial Arts has allowed me to travel to numerous places such as Grambling (Ruston) LA, Longview TX, and Memphis TN. I was able to meet

TRAINING INFORMATION

- Martial Arts Styles & Rank: Eclectic Karate - Black Belt, -Five Animal Style Kung Fu - Black Sash, -Sho Tai Flow Combat - Seventh Dan, -Shotokan Karate Do - Seventh Dan, -Mind Body and Shen - Black Belt/Seventh Level
- Instructors/Influencers: William Mason, Sifu Pearl, Grandmaster Jay-Bee LaPuppet, Grandmaster Matthew Trimmer, Grandmaster Derrick Trent
- Birthdate: September 1, 1956
- Birthplace/Growing Up: New York City, NY
- Yrs. In the Martial Arts: 51 years
- Yrs. Instructing: 51 years
- Instructor, Co-founder of Mind Body and Shen School

PROFESSIONAL ORGANIZATIONS

- Mind Body and Shen
- Shotokan Karate Do
- United Nations of Martial Arts
- United Warriors Association

different people from all walks of life and a few celebrities, Grandmaster Cynthia Rothrock, Grandmaster Ronald Duncan, Grandmaster Ron Van Clief, and Michael Jai White.

BIO

I have over 50 years of experience in martial arts. As a child, my father and mother enrolled me in the Fordham University Sports Program. My father brought home a book called Defending yourself with Ketsugo. The book contained various martial arts styles. I practiced these exercises and techniques every day. One day, a new kid moved into my neighborhood, and he was a martial artist. He started teaching me when I was 13 years old. I was interested in other sports as well and taught him basketball in return for his martial arts skills. When I started protecting the younger kids from the older ones, that's when I decided to take martial arts seriously. I started teaching many kids what I had learned. I believe I got started in martial arts to help people and show them a better way to live mentally and physically. I studied eclectic karate under Sensei William Mason as well as various styles of Kung Fu under Sifu Pearl. In 1989, I was certified by the Dallas Texas Institute of Aerobic Technology. I competed in various martial arts tournaments as well as taught martial arts in various locations, such as Grambling State University, Lincoln University (PA), and Bronx Public School #151.

PERSONAL ACHIEVEMENTS

- B.A. in Liberal Arts from College of New Rochelle
- Participated in the NBA Pro-Am/Basketball League
- Invitation for United States Basketball Tryouts (Staten Island Stallions)

MAJOR ACHIEVEMENTS

- National Youth Sports Program Appreciation Award (2002)
- Lifetime Appreciation Award from Mind Body and Shen (2005 & 2007)
- Tai Chi Hall of Fame Certificate of Martial Arts Dedication (2007)
- The American Shotokan Appreciation Award (2008)
- Induction into the Action Martial Arts Hall of Honors (2009)
- Action Martial Arts Magazine Award for Exemplary Dedication to The Martial Arts for 35+ Years (2009)
- Exemplary Contributions as an Ambassador to The Martial Arts (2010)
- Goodwill Ambassador to The Martial Arts (2013)
- Platinum Contribution to The Martial Arts (2015)
- Esteem Martial Artist Award (2019)
- 50 years Dedication to The Martial Arts (2020)
- AMAA Who's Who Legends Award (2020)

One of my greatest accomplishments was cofounding The Mind, Body and Shen Organization. Martial arts have impacted my life in various ways, such as an increased knowledge of dealing with people inside and outside of the arts. My thought process is diplomatic and open and has put me in the position to be recognized in books and magazines; I even wrote an article for Action Martial Arts Magazine in 2008.

Bill "Superfoot" Wallace

The entire world knows him as SUPERFOOT! He was featured on the Cover of Who's Who Legends 2017 with his brother in arms original world light heavyweight champion Jeff Smith and friends Joe Corley and Bill Clark. Five + decades after he started martial arts, Bill Wallace is a Grand Master Instructor and one of the global martial arts world's most influential personalities.

Grand Master Wallace was born in Portland, Indiana, and trained in wrestling during his high school years. He began his study of Judo in 1966 and was forced to discontinue his Judo related activities because of an injury he suffered to his right knee during practice. He then began to study Shorin-ryu Karate under Michael Gneck in February 1967, while serving in the U.S. Air Force.

Wallace was a prolific point fighter, and he won tournaments all over North America and fought on the US teams competing internationally. An injury to his right knee forced him to abandon kicking with that leg and he perfected kicking with the left leg. Clocked at nearly 60 miles an hour, he was perennially ranked as the premiere kicker in the country and among the top 10 fighters by all ratings services.

In September, 1974 the Professional Karate Association (PKA) emerged and held the world's first Full Contact Karate Championship in the LA Sports Arena. Bill Wallace was chosen to represent the Untied States and emerged as the world's first Full

Contact Middleweight Champion on ABC's Wide World of Entertainment.

Honing in on his incredible speed and accuracy, he was nicknamed Superfoot, a moniker that became synonymous with Bill Wallace the world over. Superfoot's first title defense was against Atlanta's Joe Corley at the 1975 Battle of Atlanta, where he captured his first defense win in 9 rounds. As a result of his incredible reputation, CBS signed Wallace for quarterly live title defenses, and in 1977 they also signed Joe Corley to be the expert commentator for the Superfoot bouts. Superfoot would continue winning and would retire live on CBS in 1980, one of the few fighters who stayed retired and remained undefeated at 23-0.

The PKA promoted the sport of full-contact karate on NBC, CBS and ESPN. PKA Full-contact karate differed from Muay Thai style kickboxing in that leg kicks were allowed in kickboxing and forbidden in full-contact karate. Wallace, the epitome of high kicking, joined Joe Corley on ESPN for the Defense and Fitness Tips of the Week, where Wallace showed world-class athletes from golf, basketball, baseball, football and track the proper ways to use the sponsor's Power Stretch machine to improve their athletic performance and prevent injuries. Wallace and Corley together inspired thousands of viewers to join karate schools through their series.

In 1990 Bill Wallace (166 lbs) fought one last exhibition kickboxing/karate match with friend Joe Lewis (198 lbs) on pay per view. Both Wallace and Lewis were refused a boxing license because of their age. The exhibition ended with one judge in favor for Wallace, another in favor for Lewis, and the third judge scored the

bout a tie, ending the exhibition in a draw.

Wallace has taught karate, judo, wrestling and weight lifting at Memphis State University. The author of a college textbook about karate and kinesiology, he continues to teach seminars across the United States and abroad.

He was the arch nemesis of long-time friend Chuck Norris in A Force of One. His other film credits include Kill Point, with Cameron Mitchell, Continental Divide and Neighbors, with John Belushi; The Protector, with Jackie Chan; Los Bravos with Hector Echavarria; A Prayer for the Dying, with Mickey Rourke; Ninja Turf; and Sword of Heaven.

Wallace was the play-by-play commentator for the inaugural Ultimate Fighting Championship pay-per-view event in 1993 alongside fellow kickboxer Kathy Long and NFL Hall of Famer Jim Brown.

Wallace administers an organization of karate schools under his "Superfoot" system, all members of the PKA WORLDWIDE Associated Schools.

He was elected to Black Belt Magazine's Hall of Fame in 1973 as "Tournament Karate Fighter of the Year" and again in 1978 as "Man of the Year", has appeared on magazine covers the world over and still today is one of the most sought after instructors in the world.

SUPERFOOT: a Martial Arts Legacy for All Time!

Johnny Warren

"Martial Arts are a big part of who I am and what I have become: a leader and a teacher..."

Martial arts not only gave me the opportunity to fight and become a world champion, but they are also a big part of who I am and what I have become: a leader and a teacher. It will always be in my life.

BIO

Not a typical bullied kid, but growing up as a small child in a very aggressive manner due to being born in a war-torn country at that time (Vietnam) to an American soldier and a Vietnamese mother. I was always looked at as an odd kid and the enemy because of my father, who was an American soldier fighting in Vietnam and because I would never back down from a fight. My My Vietnamese uncle started training me so I could protect myself and have a venue to release my aggression. Even when I was younger, I always wanted to fight and become a fighter.

TRAINING INFORMATION

- Martial Arts Styles & Rank: WarKwanDo (8th Dan/ Hachidan) "GM", KiDoKwan (8th Dan/Hachidan) "GM", Vovinam (2nd Dan/Nidan), Kongo-Do (1st Dan/Shodan), Kyokushin (1stDan/Shodan), Okinawan Shorin-ryu (1stDan/Shodan)
- Instructors/Influencers: Nguyen Van Tuoi, Akira Hachirou, Harold Diamond, Chuck Daily, Larry Shepard, Conrado P. Alvarado
- Birthdate: March 2, 1969
- Birthplace/Growing Up: Saigon, Vietnam / Panama City Beach, FL / San Francisco, CA
- Yrs. In the Martial Arts: 50 years
- Yrs. Instructing: 30 years
- School owner, Manager & Instructor

PROFESSIONAL ORGANIZATIONS

- WarKwanDo
- KiDoKwan
- Kongo-Do

PROFESSIONAL ORGANIZATIONS

- PKA World Wide
- American Martial Arts Alliance
- Sports Karate Museum History General
- USA Martial Arts Hall of Fame

PERSONAL ACHIEVEMENTS

- Grand-Master/Director/President of KiDoKwan System and promoted to 8th Dan/Hachidan before the passing of his first instructor- Nguyen Van Tuoi.
- Owner/Director/President/GrandMaster of the WarKwando system, which continues to grow. With his students taking it to another level on both the sport aspect and Martial Arts community.
- Raising two boys as a single parent and passing the Martial Arts to them.

MAJOR ACHIEVEMENTS

- IKBO World Jr. Lightweight Champion
- IKBA World Lightweight Champion
- ISKA US Regional Featherweight Champ
- ISKA Colorado State Bantamweight Champion
- IKBF North American Bantamweight Champion
- Colorado State Point/Kata Grand Champion

Don Warrener

"I still thank my instructors for the royal beatings I received at the end of their fists and feet..."

BIO

My martial arts career began on March 15, 1966 in Hamilton, Ontario in Canada. My teacher in Canadian Karate was Benny Allen who trained the best of the best fighters in Canada including Wally Slocki and Teddy Martin. I still thank them for the royal beatings I received at the end of their fists and feet. I was promoted to Shodan two years to the day after I started.

In 1973 my teacher then introduced me to Richard Kim and I soon became his student. Over my years in the martial arts I also received instruction from Morio Higaonna, Gogen "The Cat" Yamaguchi, Joe Lewis, Frank Lee, Dr. Dom Lopez, and Wally Jay to name but a few.

In 1977 I started one of Canada's most successful magazines, "The Voice of the Martial Arts."

In 1980 I started a publishing company, Masters Publishing, and it's still going strong today.

TRAINING INFORMATION

- Belt Ranks & Martial Arts Styles: Shodan, Canadian Karate
- Instructors/Influencers: Benny Allen, Wally Slocki, Teddy Martin
- Birthdate: 1960-ish
- Birthplace/Growing Up: Canada
- Yrs. In the Martial Arts: 55 years
- School Owner, Manager, Instructor, Martial Arts Author, Member PKA Worldwide

In 1985 I restored one of the most significant historical buildings with over 20,000 square feet as a martial arts school. This structure, the Hamilton Custom House, was previously owned and built by Queen Victoria at a cost of over $1 million dollars. I've also received certificates honoring me from the federal government for my efforts.

That done, I then started to establish the largest chain of schools in Canada and have over 33 schools opened with 103 franchises sold and an enrollment of over 9000 students.

In 1998 I made a radical jump and relocated to sunny Los Angeles, California. There I started a video production company, Rising Sun Productions, and today the library has over 1800 titles available in it. My publishing company now has more than 123 titles, and I personally have written over 23 books on martial arts.

Douglas Wong

"I've seen how martial arts has shaped my children into responsible adults and role models for thousands of fans around the world."

BIO

I was raised in South Central Los Angeles (Watts). I learned to defend myself and general interest in all martial arts systems. I have learned numerous tips from various martial artists from all systems while interviewing them for various magazine articles. We ran Inside Kung Fu Magazine, part of my brother's media company for 37 years before we sold it to a New York company. I still receive numerous letters from fans worldwide. I've been asked to appear and speak at numerous Martial Arts events around the world. I've seen how martial arts has shaped my children into responsible adults and role models for thousands of fans around the world. It helped me in the entertainment business, from the original Movie of the Week "Kung Fu" in 1971 to the present, where my son, Travis Wong, is one of the top stunt and fight coordinators in the business. My daughter, Tia Wong Katoa, is the V.P. of Production for Nick Cannon's

TRAINING INFORMATION

- Martial Arts Styles & Rank: Five Animal Kung Fu (Ng Ying Ga) Black Sash; Five Family Style (Ng Ga Kin); Black Sash; Five Animal Style - Instructor Level; Soft Hand Style (Yau Kung Mon) Brown Sash); Lima Lama (Hand of Wisdom) Black Belt; Wing Chun Kung Fu (Beautiful Springtime) Black Sash; White Tiger Kung Fu System (Bak Fu Pai) Black Sash; Taoist Elixir Style (Tao-On Pai) Instructor; White Lotus Kung Fu (Bai Ling Ga) Grandmaster- Si-Gung and Sijo founder of system
- Instructors/Influencers: GM Ark Yuey Wong, GM Share K. Lew, Master Haumea "Tiny" Lefiti, GM Tino Tuiolosega, Dr. Andrew Ming, GM Richard Wan, Master Walter Wong
- Birthdate: December 7, 1948
- Birthplace/Growing Up: Los Angeles, CA
- Yrs. In the Martial Arts: 61 years
- Yrs. Instructing: 53 years
- School owner, Manager & Instructor

PROFESSIONAL ORGANIZATIONS

- Member of Sil Lum Kung Fu Assn.
- AAU Chinese Martial Arts Division as the Association Chinese Martial Arts Chairperson for Southern CA.
- Regional Chairperson for Pacific Region in May 1992
- National Vice Chairmen of the United States in Sept. 1992

entertainment company. Now I will start training my grandson with my daughter, Cassidy Wong Bigham. My wife still teaches 6 days a week of Kung Fu and Tai Chi classes. She continues to act and teach in various senior citizen programs.

PROFESSIONAL ORGANIZATIONS

- National AAU Life Member since July 1992
- Member of International Teachers Association of the Martial Arts [ITAMA]
- Founding member of United Kung Fu Federation of North America
- Adviser to USA Wu Shu-Kung Fu Federation
- Member of World Head of Family Sokeship Council
- Former member of National Association of Professional Martial Artists [NAPMA]
- Senior Board of Credentials and Specialty Consultants at Martial Science University
- Martial Art Consultant at Martial Arts History Museum
- Senior Advisor at Whipping Willow Association
- Martial Art Consultant at White Lotus Training Center

PERSONAL ACHIEVEMENTS

- Commendations and Resolutions: California State Senate and Assembly, Governor of Calif., L.A. City Council, Office of L.A. Mayor, San Diego Mayor, L. A. City Council and County Board of Supervisors, U.S. Marine Corps, American Red Cross, Lion International, Save the Children Foundation, Ethiopian Famine Relief Project, Kiwanis, Rotary International, Make A Wish Foundation; and many others; awarded 8th degree Black Belt and title of Professor in American Teachers Association of the Martial Arts [ATAMA] 1993; listed in Who's Who in Karate and the Other Martial Arts, Who's Who in American Martial Arts, Leader of the Chinese Martial Arts, Masters, Founders and Leaders of American Martial Arts; Who's Who of ATAMA 1995; Martial Arts Source Book 1995; was chosen Employee of the Quarter April 1996, City of Los Angeles, Personnel Department; inducted into the International Martial Arts Hall of Fame in September 1997; Grandmaster of the Year World Head of Family Sokeship Council; featured in more than 500 magazines and newspaper articles including Life, Premiere, Runner's World, Interview, Natural Physique, Exercise for Men Only, American Cinematographer, Penthouse, Asiam, L.A. Times, Daily News, Variety, Inside Kung Fu, Master's & Styles, Professional Karate, Official Karate, Racquetball Illustrated, Nickelodeon, Inside Karate, Martial Arts Professional, Martial Arts Illustrated, World of Martial Arts, Black Belt, Kick Illustrated and many others.

MAJOR ACHIEVEMENTS

- Books: Kung Fu The Way of Life (was just named one of the top ten books of all time on Kung Fu; Shaolin Fighting Theories & Concepts forward by GM Eric Lee; Deceptive Hand of Wing Chun; Kung Fu The Endless Journey forward by family friend Muhammad Ali; video tape series: Shaolin Fighting Theories & Concepts, Chinese Martial Arts Fighting Skills, Chinese In-Fighting, 1992, Martial Arts Fundamental & Self Defense with Carrie Ogawa-Wong, 1992; DVD: Kung Fu with Master Wong (2005) Combat-White Lotus Kung Fu (2008) trained Jason Scott Lee for movie "Dragon - The Bruce Lee Story," 1992; trained Kevin Sorbo for TV series "The Legendary Journey of Hercules" 1993; trained Lucy Lawless for TV series "Xena, Warrior Princess," 1995; trained Allison Smith and Linden Ashby for TV series "Spy Game," 1997; trained Ryan Gosling for TV series "Young Hercules," 1998; was honored as one of Hollywood's top martial arts consultants and trainers by Wesley Snipes production of "Masters of the Martial Arts" in July 1998; in July 1999 trained Gina Torres for new television series "Cleopatra 2525" released in Jan. 2000; members of the White Lotus Association have appeared in more than 1000 major motion pictures and television shows from "Kung Fu" (movie of the week - 1972) to Blind Eye an episode on MANWSER 2010; GI Joe 2, Green Hornet, Captain America, Transformer, Dr. Strange, Pacific Rim 2 - The Uprising, Paramount's Snake Eyes: G.I. Joe Origins (2021) etc. Office/studio: White Lotus Martial Arts Center has moved to JAM Center (Joining All Movement Gym located at 18242 Sherman Way, Reseda, CA 91335 (818) 343-1615. Entrance and parking in the rear of the building. See our website at whitelotuskungfu.com; travis-wong.com.; joiningallmovement.com.

Keith Yates

"Master Yates is the longest continually teaching Tae Kwon Do / Karate instructor in the State of TX."

BIO

Keith D. Yates started his martial training in 1965 under International champion Allen R. Steen. In 1968, he became Mr. Steen's youngest black belt at the age of 17. Shortly thereafter Mr. Steen named him head-instructor at the North Dallas location of the famed Texas Karate Institute (the first commercial dojo in the entire state of Texas). GM Yates became the top forms competitor and teacher of kata for the entire chain of TKI schools. He won numerous kata tournaments including the 1971 Texas State Championships. Mr. Steen says Yates is the longest continually teaching Tae Kwon Do / karate instructor in the state of Texas. His black belt students are champions, teachers and writers.

Yates has trained with many other instructors including Skipper Mullins, Pat Burleson, Jhoon Rhee and Ted Gambordella. He also earned additional black belts in Jujutsu and kobudo. GM Yates has traveled all across the

TRAINING INFORMATION

- Belt Ranks & Martial Arts Styles: Nam Seo Kwan Taekwondo (10th Dan), Okinawan Kobudo (4th Dan), JuiJutsu (2nd Dan)
- Instructors/Influencers: Allen Steen
- Birthplace/Growing Up: TX
- Yrs. In the Martial Arts: 55 years
- Yrs. Instructing: 52 years

PROFESSIONAL ORGANIZATIONS

- American Karate and Taekwondo Organization, President
- American Karate Black Belt Association, Chairman
- Gospel Martial Arts Union, Chairman

nation as a seminar teacher and has appeared on many television and radio programs discussing the philosophy and history of the martial arts. He has authored or co-authored 14 books and to date has written over five-hundred magazine articles and columns.

His instructional videos have sold around the word and he just released a new smart-phone app on Tae Kwon Do patterns.

Yates introduced the first karate-for-credit program in the Southwest when he became an adjunct professor of physical education at Southern Methodist University in 1971. He wrote some of the curriculum for the first nationally certification program for martial arts instructors in conjunction with the Cooper Institute for Aerobics Research. He was named to the first class of the Texas Martial Arts Hall of Fame in 1995 and is in several other halls of fame. He served as contributing writer for MA Professional and MA Success Magazines and editor of Official Karate Magazine. The late Jhoon Rhee called him one of the nation's foremost authorities on Tae Kwon Do.

He did his master's thesis on the "Spiritual Aspects of the Martial Arts" at Dallas Theological Seminary where he served as adjunct professor. He is the chairman of the High-Dan Board of the American Karate Black Belt Association, one of the oldest organizations in the country; the Chairman of the Gospel Martial Arts Union; and was on the Board of Advisors for Chuck Norris's Kickstart for Kids for several years. He is the founder and

PERSONAL ACHIEVEMENTS

- Kata Champion
- Author & Teacher
- Founder and on Leadership Boards of several organizations

MAJOR ACHIEVEMENTS

- 16 books
- 500+ articles
- Introduced Karate-for-Credit curriculum in SW USA
- Longest continual-teaching instructor in Texas
- Inductee first class of the Texas Martial Arts Hall of Fame
- Inductee first class of the National Council on Martial Arts
- 10th Dan Tae Kwon Do, 4th Dan Kobudo, 2nd Dan Ju-Jutsu
- Founder: Nam Seo Kwan Taekwondo
- President: American Karate Taekwondo Organization
- Former editor, Official Karate Magazine
- Mobile App / YouTube Channel

BIO (continued)

president of the American Karate and Tae Kwon Do Organization. Keith and his wife, Linda, are the parents of four grown children and 10 grandchildren. He continues to live and teach in the Dallas area.

Elite
PUBLICATIONS